PURITY DRIVEN LIFE

God's call to character and integrity

By Mike Maxwell

Copyright 2016 by Mike Maxwell

All rights reserved. This book or any portion thereof may not be reproduced or used in any manner whatsoever without the express written permission of the publisher except for the use of brief quotations in a book review.

Printed in the United States of America

First Printing, 2016

www.thepuritydrivenlife.org

When it comes to sexual sin...
"What has been done will be done again;
There is nothing new under the sun."
Ecclesiastes 1:9

Book 8, The confessions of St. Augustine, written 398 A.D.

Bound I was, not with another man's irons, but by my own iron will. My will the enemy held, and thence had made a chain for me, and bound me. For of forward will, was lust made; and lust served became custom; and custom not registered became necessity. By which links, as it were joined (whence I called it a chain) a hard bondage held me enthralled.

Book of Proverbs (5:1-14), King Solomon, written 900 B.C.

"...pay close attention to this... what I tell you will keep you out of trouble. The lips of a seductive woman are oh so sweet; her soft words are oh so smooth. But it won't be long before she's gravel in your mouth, a pain in your gut, a wound in your heart...So, my friend...don't treat my words casually. Keep your distance from such a woman; absolutely stay out of her neighborhood. You don't want to squander your wonderful life, to waste your precious life...You don't want to end your life full of regrets, nothing but sin and bones...Saying, "Oh, why didn't I do what they told me? Why did I reject a disciplined life? ...My life is ruined!" (MSG Bible)

A Modern Tale, written 2013 A.D.

Here's a tale of deceit and intrigue,
had by most but few can see,
a serpent lies in wait to have you,
speaking honey traps.
He spins a tale of love that's waiting,
just reach out and take the fruit,
all your dreams are found in her,
she's waiting just for you.
Take your fill there's always more, ah,
you've reached the golden shore,
yet in your taking you need more,
and you can't fill the hole.
Now eyes open you can see,
you've sold your soul and it was cheap,
burning coals are in your lap…
and you… have tasted hell.

IT WILL COST
YOUR LIFE!

Proverbs 7

Dedication

All my love to my amazing God and Savior Jesus Christ and his Holy Spirit who, in answer to my mother's prayers, touched me with his life transforming presence in 1993. He has my gratitude for never ceasing to love me, even when I fell into the bondage of sexual sin and for providing me with the opportunity to humble myself and choose Him again in a new and deeper way. He led me to the reality of deliverance through His word (James 5:16) and released my shame and allowed me to experience his love through his people, bringing me to a deeper intimacy with Him.

I want to thank many members of my Willamette Christian Church family and those who have witnessed and walked with me on this journey. Pastor Chris Nye and Chris Yarco who showed me true love and grace when I expected rejection. The Dale Anderson family who let me sleep on their couch; Mark and Wendi Manthey who have loved and prayed for me as long as I have known them; Darrel Farah and Dean Baskerville who loved and prayed for me. My mentors, Gregory Hasek, Nathan and all the men in the purity groups that I have shared my soul with, who accepted and encouraged me.

You are the Church in action; godly men and women powered by the faith and love of the Holy Spirit living in you. You brought me love and encouragement in the battle. I am grateful for you. You inspire me. It has been, and is an honor to fight with you by my side. Thank you for all you have given me.

Introduction

Why did I write this book?

I can truly say I have never had a burning personal desire to convey any sense of expertise in the area of sexual sin. Moreover, I am not excited at the prospect of those who know me now, or knew me in my past, learning that sexual sin is something I have had to deal with.

When I found myself fighting this battle, only to lose everything I held most dear, my wife and daughter, feeling exposed before friends and relatives, and left only with God, I begged Him not to abandon me as well. I told Him I was willing to become a fool before all men if He still wanted to make something of my life. He has been utterly faithful, and my heart's desire is to obediently, and faithfully serve Him every moment of my remaining days, however long that may be.

I am not a professional writer, and in the end, it may be that this book is simply a venue for my personal healing. However, I pray that it provides a deeper and broader work among the men and women in the Church, both those who struggle with similar issues and those who are called as the Apostle Peter was, to strengthen their brothers. (Luke 22:32).

On some level, I think we all know that God is ultimately our greatest and purest desire; however, it often takes bitter winter seasons to open our eyes to this reality. Many times, God must allow us to feel a great deal of pain in order to lift the fog of sin's deceit. I thank God He loves you and me enough to reveal the truth and reality of that love to us, no matter how painful the process. I am grateful He disciplines those He loves. In hindsight, I would not trade a single painful moment for all I have gained.

My sincere hope and prayer is, and has been, that you read this book under the power of the Holy Spirit's leading. That you willingly submit to God's loving conviction and experience a deep hunger for his holiness to manifest itself in your life. If God uses this book to awaken you to reality, I am grateful to have been a participant in the process.

I greatly desire that you heed the warnings God has laid out for his children in the area of sex, lust and immorality, and as a result, are able to take prudent steps to avoid the pain that sexual sin will bring upon you. I pray that your wife and children will never experience the consequences and suffering that result from a father and husband's sexual sin.

This is not a book for the faint of heart. I have written it for men who fervently want to be the man, leader, warrior and lover that God envisioned for you as his child before the foundation of this world.

I have not sugarcoated the stark reality of this message in any way and some of what you read *should* sting as you realize how your selfish choices have and will affect your life and the lives of those for which you are responsible.

I know this may sound over-dramatic, but this message should be a spiritual slap in the face that gets your attention. Better this than the devastation you will face when your marriage and family fall apart due to your failure to be a genuine, God-pursuing disciple of Christ. Your daily choices have eternal consequences. It is time to stand up and be the godly man you were born again to be.

This book is a call to WAR!

The Purity Driven Life

Table of Contents

Chapter 1   Whitewashed

Chapter 2   Dying for a shortcut

Chapter 3   What's in a Tsunami?

Chapter 4   Did I just choose Eve?

Chapter 5   Worship what!?

Chapter 6   Programmed to salivate

Chapter 7   Shadows of freedom

Chapter 8   The desert is meant to kill you!

Chapter 9   Killing fleas

Chapter 10   Obedience matters

Chapter 11   What is truth?

Chapter 12   Jesus shares a secret

Chapter 13   Is it in you?

Chapter 14   Enter the battle Part 1

Chapter 15   Enter the battle Part 2

Chapter 16   Abiding

A Note to Shepherds of God's sheep

THE PURITY DRIVEN LIFE

God's call to character and integrity

Chapter 1 | Whitewashed

"The temptation of the age is to look good without being good."[1]

"Woe to you…you hypocrites! You are like whitewashed tombs, which look beautiful on the outside but on the inside you are full of…everything unclean…you appear to people as righteous but on the inside you are full of hypocrisy and wickedness." (Matt 23:27-28)

Several years ago, there was a popular television show called "Dexter." The title is based on the name of the lead character, who works as a respectable "blood splatter analyst" for the Miami Metro homicide unit. However, Dexter has a dark secret. He has a compulsion to commit what we would consider one of the most seriously abhorrent crimes against humanity; he is a serial killer. Dexter refers to his compulsion as his "dark passenger."

As the plot develops, we learn that Dexter's desire to kill other living beings is the result of traumatic events in his early childhood that have left an indelible stamp on his psyche. During Dexter's early teen years, his adoptive father, a police officer, begins to notice that something is developmentally wrong with him. Wanting to protect his son from the consequences of acting on his desire to kill, he teaches Dexter that society will not condone this type of behavior.

Dexter intellectually accepts that his desires are morally wrong and understands that society has penalties for this type of behavior, but this knowledge does not change his desire. Recognizing that Dexter cannot control his appetite, his father develops a code of conduct with a specific set of rules for Dexter to operate within. These rules allow Dexter to satiate his desire to murder other human beings AND justify his behavior. This code helps him avoid discovery and remain hidden in plain sight.

Dexter lives by a philosophy that bridles his desire and minimizes the harm of his actions to society, at least in his mind. Dexter channels his compulsion to kill into hunting down and murdering other serial killers. He justifies his actions by believing those he kills are criminals who deserve to die because of their crimes against humanity.

I admit I was immediately hooked on the show. As the season progressed, I almost found myself agreeing that if Dexter cannot overcome his desire to kill, then channeling it this way is the best way to control it. In fact, it wasn't long before I found myself hoping Dexter was able to avoid getting caught!

About the time I began watching Dexter, I was also beginning to recognize and wrestle with my own "dark passenger," a compulsion for sexual sin. I was becoming painfully aware that it was controlling me. I found myself unable to rid myself of lustful thoughts and actions and it seemed to be getting worse. I could relate to Dexter's uncontrollable drive and his need to satiate his desires. I too had justified my actions and channeled them towards what I thought were least harmful to others and my marriage, pornography. Like Dexter, I was hiding in plain sight, in the Church. The analogy was striking and statistics regarding sexual sin tell me there is a very good chance you are hiding in Church as well.

Awareness is a beginning

My hope is that you picked up this book because you recognize you have a sexual sin issue coming between you and your relationship with God. It is affecting your other important relationships as well, including your marriage, your children and the authenticity of your male friendships. My hope is that you have arrived at the point where you want to deal with this deadly sin God's way and begin pursuing a holy life.

If that is the case, you probably already know that wanting to stop unwanted sexual thoughts, along with the resulting behavior, and actually doing it are not even close to being the same thing. The old saying "the road to hell is paved with good intentions" is a wise saying for a good reason. There is a spiritual battle within us and it seems that we often lose to the desires of the flesh, regardless of what we claim to want.

The Apostle Paul, who wrote most of the New Testament and gave his life out of love for Christ wrote the following.

"I am a creature of the flesh [carnal, un-spiritual], having been sold into slavery under [the control of] sin. For I do not understand my own actions [I am baffled, bewildered]. I do not practice or accomplish what I wish, but I do the very thing that I loathe [which my moral instinct condemns]. (Romans 7:14, 15 AMPC)

As a Christian man, this passage describes perfectly the very battle raging within us. We might hate this sin and what it compels us to do, but our sin impassions us. It medicates us and at the same time, we feel alive, at least temporarily. However, giving in to these passions come with a steep price. We are constantly ashamed because our actions do not match what the Bible says should flow from the heart of a godly man of character.

This is what Paul describes as a carnal Christian. As Christian men, we call ourselves by the name of Christ, and say we are his disciples, but our lives do not bear the fruit of a real relationship with Him. We claim to be his sons but our hearts are nothing like his.

"It's one thing not to sin; it's another not to want to!"

~ Jacquelyn K. Heasley ~

Our Christian shortcomings may not be readily apparent to others by simply looking at us. In appearance, we might look the part of the dutiful Christian. We say the right words, regularly attend Church, and maybe even volunteer to serve in a ministry. We may look the part and have others fooled, but in our heart, we know the sins we embrace when no one is looking. We are slaves to a "dark passenger." Despite having been bought with the precious blood of Christ, we are still slaves to sin; filled with shame and afraid to admit it to those around us. As a result, we hide our true selves and project a false image out of fear that we will be rejected, condemned or even considered unlovable.

A cardboard foundation

Several years ago, I went to the movie theater on a date. We purchased our giant beverages and were on our way down the hall to the theater when my date let me know she needed to visit the restroom. I occupied myself by pacing the dimly lit hallway observing the wall posters and watching couples and families come and go.

Have you ever noticed those full-sized cardboard displays of an upcoming movie in the hallway? Well, there was one of those nearby. It had a square base about 2 ½ feet high with the glossy cardboard characters mounted atop in their action poses. I wandered over, absent-mindedly inspected it, then turned to do some people watching as one of the movies finished and moviegoers began to fill the hallway. Without thinking, I decided to sit down on the display behind me while I waited.

What happened next reminds me of that grade school prank where, just as you have fully committed to sitting down in your tiny plastic chair, the class bully kicks it away without your knowing and you hit the floor full force! As my butt went down, the display gave way, crumpling like an empty box (which it was). My arms and feet went up, but somehow I managed to maintain ahold of my beverage without spilling a drop. I guess I am more athletic than bright! I immediately jumped up and nonchalantly looked around to see if anyone had seen the incident. Amazingly, although the hall was filled with people, no one seemed to take notice! I quietly wandered away from the display, acting like nothing had happened.

For a Christian man to have the life God offers us, our lives have to be genuine, more than a façade that projects a false spirit of holiness and righteousness. There can be no victory or true joy when we have hidden sin in our lives. When we harbor unconfessed sin we are simply going through the motions of Christianity. We might delude ourselves into thinking that God's blessing and presence are with us. We may profess his name, have material blessings and look the part of a Christian. However, when it comes time for a real spiritual fight, a failing marriage, the loss of your career, the loss of a dream or maybe something as serious as your child being diagnosed with terminal cancer, we are forced to confront the harsh reality that our inward walk with God may not be as solid as it appears from the outside. When we are tested, we find that we have no foundation and are forced to admit that our Christianity is a nothing more than a hollow cardboard cutout of the Christian life, empty of any real relationship with Jesus.

Sin Management

We need to recognize and acknowledge that something is not right with our Christianity if we are more committed to *managing* our sin than ensuring our death to its hold over us. Perseverance in our daily dying to sin is the walk destined for the Christian man, but how is this done, specifically as it relates to sexual sin?

When we first get saved, we usually began wrestling with sexual sin in the power of our flesh, in our own will power; and oftentimes we have a measure of success... for a time. We may begin to get confident, thinking that we have overcome it, but eventually our sinful desires come back and we continue to struggle. It is very common to come to a point of resignation regarding our inability to overcome sexual sin that leads down one of three paths.

1. We stop fighting our desires, give up, backslide and eventually lose or reject the Christian faith; believing it to be powerless to affect any real change in our lives.

2. We resign ourselves to sin, and a life of hiding our sin; believing a chain of lies something along the following:

- It is impossible to defeat this sin.
- God knew I couldn't defeat it, that's why He died for me.
- I will only be free from this sin when Christ returns.
- I am under grace so... it's ok.

This path is a particularly deceitful train of thought that leads to where most Christian men trapped in sexual sin have settled today. It is easy to see why, especially for results oriented, get it done before the sun goes down American types. If the word of God says, "Sin shall not have dominion over you" (Romans 6:14) and yet it still does, then we tend to reinterpret what "shall not have dominion over you" means and our conclusion is something like this.

"Since I can't overcome this sin, and God knows I have tried, sin not having dominion over me must not refer to the here and now. It must somehow refer to being free from sin and temptation when Christ comes to take me to heaven. My pastor teaches that Christ died as payment for my sins. That must not only be for past sins but all the sins I would ever commit, even those I commit after accepting Christ. Jesus surely did that because He knew I would continue to sin so… as long as I express remorse afterward, then it is probably ok and I am good with God. After all, we are under grace and we wouldn't need a savior if we could overcome the sin of lust."

So like Dexter, we begin to "manage" our sin, trying to minimize its effects and hide it from discovery by those around us. Just as what occurred with Adam's sin in the garden, this has several inevitable effects.

- It alienates us from God as we seek to avoid his convicting presence.

- It alienates us from those closest to us as we attempt to hide behind "fig leaves" of our own making to avoid being exposed.
- It feeds our selfish desires, which are never fully satiated and inevitably grow as we resign ourselves to the control of sin.

The best lies of our enemy are those that are the easiest to swallow, those that contain a grain of truth but are an incomplete truth or a truth corrupted by just a touch of untruth. This is our enemy's specialty and this train of thought, from the standpoint of the devil, is an effective beauty. Those of us who have come to this conclusion and stay in the Church end up having a form of Godliness, but the power of God is not present (2 Timothy 3:5). Our lives, in effect are no different from the world, other than we have "branded" ourselves Christian.

We become the "Christian brand" of worldliness, and that is what we end up trying to sell, believing all you have to do is parrot a salvation prayer and viola, you are free from the consequence of sin. Even the world sees the emptiness of this kind of Christianity. This is the trap the majority of Christian men are currently snared in. The ultimate result of this thinking is now coming upon the Church; pressure to tolerate and embrace all types of sin under the guise of Church growth, inclusion and grace.

3. The third option is to recognize that although Jesus paid for our sin debt *and our deliverance from its power,*

we are not meant, or expected to escape the bondages of sin in our lives through our efforts alone.

As a result, we choose in faith to *desperately pursue* the power of the Holy Spirit to fill and empower us. We begin to wrestle *not with our sin directly, but with our spirit in submission and surrender to God.* We begin seeking to yield to his love and power to work in us, rather than yielding to our love for sin.

I know as you read this you may be saying, "I don't understand what that means. How does this actually happen? What do I need to do?" I know you have many questions, and this book is my attempt to answer them. I will try to share what it looks like to work this out in your daily life and to explain why it is imperative that you do so.

First, I ask you to consider this question. Are you serious about dealing with sin in your life and getting right with God? Or, are you simply wanting to placate your conscious by "doing something" that looks productive so you can comfort yourself into believing that you attempted to be obedient to God?

Americans are notorious for engaging in activity and distraction to avoid actually facing deep issues. That is why we have so many workaholics, video gamers, fitness addicts and all the other "white" addictions in America. Activity deludes us into thinking and feeling as if we are being productive. We are, but often not in the area that needs addressing.

A blunt Jesus

So, I ask again, are you really serious about wanting to partner with God in dealing with your sexual sin? Are you ready to draw a line in the sand and step over it in surrender to God, no matter what you have to do? You may not realize all that an affirmative answer will entail, however there is no other way to walk as the man God has designed you to be. I know this idea can be daunting, but listen as Jesus eplains how urgent your participation in overcoming sexual sin is. Jesus bluntly says,

"If your hand causes you to sin, cut it off! It's better to enter eternal life with only one hand than to go into the unquenchable fires of hell with two hands." (Mark 9:43)

It does not get any more direct than that. Here is Jesus; fully aware of the grace his death will bring to us, instructing us to be extreme in our dealings with personal sin. *The implication in his warning is that our unwillingness to deal with sin in our life can keep us from appropriating the grace that will bring us into eternal life with Jesus.*

In addition, notice, Jesus does not say, "If your hand causes you to sin, I will cut it off for you."

I can hear you say, "But I thought we were saved by grace?" We should never lose sight of this truth. However, as we will see, the Bible teaches that we cannot interpret God's grace as an excuse for continuing in sin expecting God to look the other way no matter how convenient that would be for us.

Consider what Paul says about this subject in his letter to Christians living at Rome.

"What shall we say, then? Shall we go on sinning so that grace may increase? By no means! We are those who have died to sin; how can we live in it any longer? ...we know that our old self was crucified with Him *so that the body ruled by sin might be done away with, that we should no longer be slaves to sin...*" (Romans 6:1-6)

> "Grace does not make room for sin...
> Grace makes room for repentance."
>
> ~ Lowell Nelson ~

Is your diaper full?

God expects a maturing Christian man to gain dominion over sin. When a baby is born, we feed and care for its every need. Babies can and do get away with things that we would never tolerate from an older child, such as filling a diaper. I think we would all agree something is drastically wrong if we were still changing a child's diaper at the age of 13. If we were, we should be concerned, realizing the child is retarded. I mean that based on the medical definition, not in a derogatory way. The same is true of our spiritual growth, God has provided for, and expects us to grow and mature out of our sinful behavior by the power of His indwelling Spirit.

Jesus does not take sin lightly and requires that we do not either. Carnal Christians are baby Christians regardless of how good they look, their age, or what position they hold in the Church. Jesus' statement that we go to the extreme of cutting of the offending hand seems shocking, but we need to remember that Jesus had a way of getting right to the root and intentions of the heart. Very few men would actually go to the length of cutting off their hand to avoid sin, which is exactly the point! We like our hands; they are useful to us and help us navigate this life. Getting rid of a hand would be a huge inconvenience, something that our flesh does NOT WANT TO DO.

At the core of Jesus' statement is the following question. Are the things in your life, whatever they are, that cause you, or enable you to continue sinning, more important to you than your right standing with God? Those conveniences that trap you in the snare of sexual sin, do you love them more than Jesus who loved you so much that He was willing to die that you might have a "choice" to walk in freedom?

Jesus is telling us that to be men of holiness and character we must get radical in demolishing any sins or idols that even in the slightest way, harm or hinder our relationship with Him. What are you *willing* to do to get right with God as it relates to the sexual sin in your life?

Any real and meaningful relationship requires accountability, and prideful people do not want to be accountable, to God or anyone else. We desire to do what we want to do, however accountability is a foundational spiritual concept. We are called to *choose* whom we will serve (be accountable to) as Lord and master, and this choice is at the heart of the ***daily*** Christian walk. You must address this issue in your heart. If you are not willing to get drastic with your sin, then you need to acknowledge that you are not surrendered to Christ as Lord. There is no halfway. You cannot serve two masters (Matthew 6:24).

"It is impossible for a man to be freed from the habit of sin before he hates it..."

~ Ignatius~

I know that many men are ashamed by their continued sin, and the message of this book is not intended to pile on the condemnation. Condemnation is from our enemy. The message I want you to hear is that there is a freedom bought for you by Jesus that our enemy never wants you to see or experience. Our enemy understands this is war and he wants you to believe that you have tried everything within reason, and that freedom is not meant for you. If you believe that, you are already his prisoner of war; and I am here to tell you that you are believing a lie from the pit of hell.

Chapter 1 | Whitewashed

"Get Real" Questions for discussion with other men:

In what way can you relate to Dexter's dark passenger?

Would you consider yourself a carnal Christian? Why?

Why do you think Jesus was so blunt about our dealing with sin, knowing that He was about to die so that grace could be extended to us?

How have you engaged in the concept of "sin management"?

Chapter 2 | Dying for a Shortcut

"He is no fool who gives what he cannot keep to gain what he cannot lose."[1]

"There is a way that seems right to a man, but its end is the way to death" (Proverbs 14:10)

I do not think most of us understand how seriously God takes sexual sin. He takes it VERY, VERY seriously and so should we. Why does God take it so seriously? As I began to deal with my own sin, I came to some interesting revelations about our covenant-keeping God and sex. Ephesians 5:25 says:

"Husbands, love your wives, just as Christ loved the Church and gave Himself up for her."

Our relationship with our wives is meant to be a mirrored reflection of Christ's relationship to his bride, the Church, of which every born again believer is a part. In giving his life and dying for our sins, Jesus provided a way for us to *intimately* unite with Him by his Holy Spirit taking up residence in us. The Bible says we become one with Christ through this process,

"But whoever is united with the Lord is one with Him in Spirit." (1 Corinthians 6:17)

The Holy Spirit becomes part of us in union with our spirit as a result of this covenant relationship with Jesus Christ. In a marriage covenant, this union is mirrored through the intimate physical union of a man with his wife in consummation of the covenant wedding vows. The Bible says through this process the man and woman become one flesh.

"…a man will leave his father and his mother and be united with his wife and the two will become one flesh. So they are no longer two, but one flesh." (Mark 10:7-8)

God cannot allow his Holy Spirit to dwell in union with an unredeemed being. The process by which we were chosen as objects of his love required the greatest sacrifice on his part. He went to the universal extreme to have this spiritual union with us. Sexual union within marriage is meant to be a holy reflection of God's love and sacrifice for you and reflect the covenant relationship we have with Him.

The devil completely understands the significance of this. When we divorce sex from the marriage covenant, it no longer reflects the covenant relationship God intended for his bride; it is a subversion of God's purpose for marriage and a demeaning and devaluing of its significance as a form of honor, commitment and *worship* to God.

With that foundation in mind, let's look at some verses in context. First Corinthians 6:17-22 from the Amplified Bible is a series of verses that should be a sobering line of thought to ponder for any man who claims to be a Christian.

"But the person who is united to the Lord becomes *one spirit with Him.*" (v. 17)

If you are a child of God, you have the Holy Spirit living in you as a guarantee that you are God's child. (See 2 Cor. 1:22) You are *one Spirit* with Christ.

"Shun immorality *and* all sexual looseness [flee from impurity in thought, word, or deed]. Any other sin which a man commits is one outside the body, but he who commits sexual immorality *sins against his own body.*" (v. 18)

Sex is a gift from God for love, expression and reflection of his love for us and is intended for *only* the mate to whom God has joined you as one flesh spiritually (Gen 2:24). When you engage in sexual acts outside of God's intended purpose, you are joining your body, soul and spirit to a person or demonic spirit in defiance of your creator. In doing so, you are bringing a third party to your relationship with God and your wife. You are fracturing your own spirit and if married, that of your wife, who is spiritually joined to you. Unfortunately, just like Adam and Eve we tend to be blind to the enormous consequences of this sin. We are oblivious to the damage this sin causes to our spiritual and physical lives and to those around us until after the fact.

"Sin and the child of God are incompatible. They may occasionally meet; they cannot live together in harmony"

~John R. W. Stott~

If you are single and engaged in sexual sin, you need to realize you are cheating on your future spouse, damaging the very soul and spirit which you will one day ask her to join as one flesh. If you intend to love her as God asks you to, then you will agree she deserves a man of godly integrity and an undefiled Spirit. To be a man of integrity means not only adhering to God's moral and ethical principles (having sound moral character and honesty), it also means the state of being whole, entire, undiminished, and uncompromised spiritually. If you are regularly sharing your body, spirit or soul with anyone or anything in *any* sexual sin activity, you are fracturing and harming your spirit man. You are a man of broken integrity, lacking godly character and discipline (2 Cor 10:5, Luke 16:23-26). You are spiritually broken by your willing sinfulness and cannot be entering a marriage covenant in true love as the spiritual leader God desires for your future bride (Ephesians 5:25-30).

If you love, truly love the woman God is giving you or is going to give you, then you will deal with your sin decisively before you take responsibility for her and say the hollow words, "vowing to forsake **ALL others so long as you both shall live** (that means even before you meet her)." If you choose to go forward in marrying her without dealing with your sin, you should not deceive yourself. As you stand there making a vow to her (and to God) to walk in this covenant relationship as God intends, you are entering your marriage based on a foundation of lies, to both your wife and the God of the universe. If you are able to do this without any spirit of remorse, it speaks volumes as to the condition of your heart and character.

"Do you not know that *your body is the temple (the very sanctuary) of the Holy Spirit* who lives within you, whom you have received [as a Gift] from God? You are not your own," (v. 19)

If you are saved, when you engage in sexual sin, by your own choice *you are forcing the Holy Spirit who lives in you to join in your sin with you!* The verse that precedes this section of scripture (v. 16) says, "Do you not know that he who unites himself with a prostitute is one with her in body? For it is said; The two will become one flesh.'"

God says that if you are his, then his Spirit lives in you and you are one with Him. He has joined his Spirit to your Spirit. When you engage in sexual sin, whether with another person, while viewing pornography, or even fantasizing with lustful intent (Matt 5:28), you force the Holy Spirit to join you because your body is His temple.

The ultimate goal of the enemy is not for us to have all kinds of fun sex; our joy is not his concern. His goal is to tempt us into sexual sin outside of God's intended covenant relationship. He desires to pervert marriage's reflection of God's love and relationship with his Church.

Getting a Spirit-filled Christian to engage in sex outside of God's plan is the consummation of a sin against the very soul of the Christian whose spirit is one with God. It is also an attack on the very Spirit of God Himself, with our willing consent. I would suggest to you that forcing the Spirit of God to participate in our sexual sin is perhaps the most self-seeking and ungrateful thing we could possibly do as a Christian!

You were bought with a price [purchased with preciousness and paid for, [made His own]. So then, honor God *and* bring glory to Him *in your body*. (v. 20)

"Repentance of the evil act, and not of the evil heart, is like men pumping water out of a leaky vessel, but forgetting to stop the leak. Some would dam up the stream, but leave the fountain still flowing."

~ Charles Spurgeon ~

The issue that Jesus wants us to see is the true condition of our heart. Our repentance should be to acknowledge that we have a heart that loves sin more than we love God, and then **repent of our heart condition. Sin is the symptom, our heart is the problem.** We have been bought by God, and if we have given our lives to God we are expected to live in progressive victory. However, this is impossible without transformed heart desires!

We will talk about strategy in more detail later in the book, but a critical step is to acknowledge our heart issues out loud by humbling ourselves, confessing our sin to God AND other trustworthy Christian men. This is where freedom, restoration and healing begin. James 5:16 tells us:

"Therefore confess your sins to each other and pray for each other *so that you may be healed.*"

I realize that actually doing this may be very difficult. For many male egos it might be easier to actually cut off your hand, but as Christian men we are called to a narrow path. We are called to do the hard things and denying our flesh is hard! It is our responsibility to our God, our families and the body of Christ, the Church. You must consider that if your pride is so great that it keeps you from being *willing* to be obedient to God in humbling yourself before other Christian men then you are in serious spiritual danger.

The Bible tells us in Proverbs 14:12 (and this is applicable to sexual sin),

"There is a way that seems right to a man, but in the end it leads to death."

What to the natural man seems like the best way to deal with our sin, committing to try harder, hiding it, handling it on our own, justifying it and all the other lies we tell ourselves to avoid doing it God's way does not work...in the long run. They are the wrong answer; they are the wrong path, a deceitful detour leading us to death.

In the walk of the Christian man, God will ask you every day "Do you trust me enough to live life my way, or are you going to say 'NO Lord' and take the path offered by your own logic and reasoning that leads to death?" Having been where you are I can hear you saying, "I've tried, but I can't live this kind of life. I fail every time and then I feel worse than ever. I hate that this sin has such control over me, but I just cannot live without giving in to sexual sin and lust! There is just no way!"

A desirable shortcut

I get it! I actually told God (literally) that I thought I would DIE if I wasn't getting my sexual needs met on the schedule I deemed appropriate. In hindsight, this seems so silly. Clearly, no man has ever died from lack of orgasm but that is what sin does to us. Fear dictates and controls our thinking.

In our pride and self-centeredness we seek to get our needs (and wants) met by taking the shortcut offered by the enemy of our soul. He *always* offers a shortcut. Even when tempting Jesus on the mount, his temptations were all offers for Jesus to circumvent God's will for Him, an offer of a shortcut. (Matthew 4:1-11). Our God loves you and me more than we can possibly conceive and has promised to provide for our every need. It is when we get our needs confused with our wants that we start to walk a slippery slope. Combine this confusion of wants and needs with a failure to trust that God really has promised to meet and provide for all our needs and we get in serious trouble.

I have learned the hard way; **there are no shortcuts for a true child of God.** The most direct route to all of God's blessing and joy is to do it all God's way, even if we do not fully understand. Satan offers a way that looks like a legitimate alternative, but in the end; at best, it is nothing but a painful detour. At worst, it could lead to the very destruction of not only your marriage, your children and your life, but also your very soul.

To straighten out our lives we have to come back to the beginning of all things, to God himself, our creator. Whether you are saved or not, this is the place to start. When your car breaks down, it makes sense to take it to the dealer for service and repair. We don't take it to the guy who does our taxes or call a plumber.

The question for you today is not *are you able* to live God's way, but are you *willing* to stop taking the shortcuts and do it God's way? If so, that is what this book is about. If you are *willing*, put your hand in the hand of our savior and choose right now to set aside your pride, humble yourself and pray for God, right now to begin this work in you today. Pray this out loud...

Dear God,

"I do love you. If I haven't fully surrendered my life to you and even if I have, I willfully choose to do so again, right now. I know that there are parts of me that love my sin and find great pleasure in it. I acknowledge that my human nature wants desperately to hold onto my sin.

But God, regardless of what my emotions, my body and my senses are telling me right now, I voluntarily choose to give you unreservedly my body, mind, soul, spirit and will for an intimate relationship with you. Fill me with your love and the tangible presence of your Holy Spirit and make me hungry for intimacy with you.

Holy Spirit, I ask you to help me sense and feel the pain and hurt that my Savior feels whenever I break his heart by choosing sinful behavior over Him. I ask you to line my heart desires up with God's heart desires and his will for me as a man surrendered to Him.

Break my heart with my sin that I might desire to do and obediently perform all that you ask of me.

Amen.

Now keep reading....

Chapter 2 | Dying for a Shortcut

"Get Real" Questions for discussion with other men:

How do you respond after knowing that your marriage is to be a reflection of God's love relationship to his Church? How would this change how you approach your marriage?

How do you feel about the idea that sexual union with your wife is a reflection of our union with the Gods Holy Spirit? Does this seem sacrilegious to you?

What tangible ways should this effect our view of sex and sexual activity?

Do you find that you repent of sin, or of a heart that loves sin? What's the difference?

What are some shortcuts you have been deceived into taking? What have been the consequences?

Chapter 3 | What's in a Tsunami?

"It is perilously easy to have amazing sympathy with God's truth and remain in sin"[1]

"...behold, you have sinned against the LORD, and be sure your sin will find you out." (Numbers 32:23)

When I finally put my pride aside and admitted that I had a problem, I had reached a point of desperation. Almost a year later, my struggle was exposed for all to see. Since then, what I found is that I am not alone in this struggle and that means neither are you. One of the most deceiving lies of our very real enemy is that you are the only one with this problem, you are different. He tells you that if people only knew the real you, they would ridicule, ostracize, cast you out and see you as being unlovable, a pervert.

Now I am not going to be so foolish as to tell you that there is no downside to facing up to the consequences of your sin. After all, they are called consequences for a reason and there is potentially unbelievable pain in the process that I cannot even begin to predict for you. However, there is also unbelievable joy, intimacy and amazing grace in the arms of our savior. Laying aside your pride will give you access to a grace that will rock your world into another dimension of love and humility if you will call on Jesus in surrender to his way of living and trust Him to walk with you every day.

Facing this issue requires character, and a true warrior of God does the right thing regardless of the ramifications. He chooses to trust that in his obedience God will take care of the consequences and be his defender and his rock. However, the enemy will do everything in his power to persuade you otherwise.

As I mentioned, not only are you are not alone in this trap, you are not even in the minority, even in the middle of Church on Sunday morning. Here are some of the most recent statistics I could find on this issue, and they might shock you.

Facts about porn in the Church: [3]

- 70% of lay leaders admit to visiting a porn site *at least once a week.*

- 50% *of Pastors* admitted the same.

- 60% of *all Christian men* (30% of Christian women) are *addicted to* porn.

- Of the 10,000 calls, emails and letters Focus on the Family receives daily, this issue represents their number one incoming request for help overall.

- 56% of divorces involve one spouse's continued use of Internet pornography. (Family Research Council, "The Effects of Pornography", 2009)

General facts about porn[3]

- 70% of men age 18-24 visit a porn site regularly
- 25% of all search requests are for porn (1 out every 4!)
- 35% of all internet downloads are porn
- 20% of men and 13% of women admit to watching porn at work
- The largest consumers of porn are 12-17 year old boys *(Let that sink in!)*
- Estimated annual Porn revenues top $14,000,000,000**

    ** More than Microsoft, Google, Amazon, eBay, Yahoo!, Apple, and Netflix combined!

You are not alone in your sexual sin, even in the Church, even if you are a woman. Sadly, the god of this world has so enticingly baited his hook that the 60% of men who claim to be filled with the Holy Spirit and sitting in our worship services each week are enslaved and suffering silently, afraid of anyone finding out for fear of loss and rejection. In the process, they stumble through the motions of having a faithful relationship to God while the devil is effectively aborting their ability to hear God's voice and believe Him for the fulfillment of their God given destinies.

No New Thing

Sexual sin is nothing new, but up until the mid-90s if you wanted pornographic material, you generally had to risk being seen buying a magazine, entering a strip club, frequenting an adult bookstore or hiring a prostitute. It had a high-level risk of being seen, caught or arrested. These risks of exposure tended to act as a fence that helped to keep our overt lusts in check and damper our ability to engage in sexual sin, at least relative to today.

With the availability of the internet in the mid-90s, access to free porn (called by some the crack cocaine of sex addiction), chat rooms and adult hookup sites began to gain entry into American homes because there was often little risk of anyone knowing if you took a little peek. Suddenly the barriers to access were gone and along with this came the testing of our spiritual character.

"Consuming pornography does not lead to more sex, it leads to more porn. Much like eating McDonald's everyday will accustom you to food that (although enjoyable) is essentially not food...

~ Virginie Despentes ~

Many Christian men, including pastors, wouldn't dream of setting foot in an adult bookstore or a massage parlor for fear of getting caught, but things have changed. The perceived risk has all but disappeared. Men who would never risk hiring a prostitute or having an affair, now have the opportunity to explore sexual sin without anyone knowing, and in complete anonymity.

Now with the internet, the perception is that "no one knows what I am doing in the privacy of my own home and I can surely hide this from my wife, my employer or the Church. So game on!"

It reminds me of the question we used to ask each other as kids, "If you knew there was no way you would ever get caught, would you steal a million dollars?" It really is a good question regarding the integrity of your character. When you know the chances of being seen or caught are low, or you are guaranteed not to get caught...the temptation is solely a pure test of character; In this case, a test of the spiritual character of the men who claim to be disciples of Jesus.

It happened so quickly

It really is amazing how quickly internet pornography penetrated our homes. The first web browser was presented to the public in 1993 and access to the web grew rapidly thereafter. By 1994, there were approximately 1 million users on the web. In 1995, Microsoft launched Windows 95 with Internet Explorer embedded in the software of almost every computer sold and use of the web began to accelerate at an exponential rate.

In 1997-1998 most of us were using modems for access and had to wait relatively long periods of time for pictures to load; but despite this inconvenience, porn was immediately a top use for internet access. In fact, in 1998 there were still only 750,000 commercial websites on the entire World Wide Web and by the year 2000 only 44% of homes in America had internet access! Around the year 2000, broadband became available to the public and we began jumping on the "broadband" wagon.

Within a few more years, by 2009, over 93% of American households had easy access to pornography in their home at lightning fast speeds.

With the risk of discovery by our Christian "peers" eliminated due to private internet access, a majority of Christian men readily embraced the promised shortcut offered by the enemy. We took the bait, hook, line and sinker, and once this door was opened it became so very difficult to close. Like a fish on a hook, we are now the devils' to control. This failure of so many Christian men says volumes about the lack of depth and integrity of our faith. We have become complacent in holiness under the excuse of "grace," and the enemy has used it against us, successfully exploiting and exposing our weakness; deeply metastasizing this cancerous tumor into the body of Christ. We must come back to the Savior to heal and restore us to become the men of integrity, the godly leaders and spiritual warriors we were called and created to be.

Becoming Numb

What I find even more frightening is that many Christian men and women who are only now seeking help for sex addiction reveal that it accelerated when many discovered internet porn during the mid to late 90s. It has taken them between 10-15 years to realize their helplessness in this area. It isn't until this cancer has become all-consuming and destroyed their spiritual life, marriages, families, relationships and careers that they have become desperate for deliverance.

"If you will not determine to be pure, you will grow more and more impure"

~ George MacDonald ~

The Bible often uses leprosy, today known as Hansen's disease, as an analogy to show the effects of sin. The analogy is extremely applicable to sexual sin. Did you know that of all the new cases of leprosy, 70% are men and 30% are women?[4] This almost exactly matches the statistics on sexual addition in the Church!

After reading the points below, I suggest you go online and look up some pictures of the effects of this disease in its advanced stages. I do not think God could have used a more devastating word picture to make his point about the effects of sin on the soul.

- Leprosy is a type of fungus caused by a bacterial infection. With increased exposure comes increased risk of contracting the disease or relapse. Just as with sexual sin, when we allow ourselves to be constantly exposed, the tendency is to take it in, to accept it, and then begin to see it as "normal." Soon it becomes a stronghold; a part of us that we can't control...what at first seemed so natural and harmless has now embedded itself in our lives.

- Children are more susceptible to leprosy due to less developed immunities, and the disease usually lies dormant in them until adulthood. In my accountability groups many of the men have childhood wounds from trauma, abuse, father wounds and parental divorce, coupled with early exposure to pornography that forms an integral part of their susceptibility to sexual temptation and addiction later on in adulthood.

- Many of those who have leprosy, especially in the early stages, show very little outward evidence of the disease. As with sexual sin, it is easy at first, to overlook and the effects seem minimal. Since we are not seeing any ill effects, we begin to minimize and justify our actions and question, "did God really say this wasn't OK? Who am I hurting?"

- The development and progression of leprosy depends largely on the level of immunity or resistance of the host. In a healthy body it can easily be defeated, but in a compromised immune system where the resistance is low it can easily gain a foothold and begin to consume the host. Sexual sin is the same way. If we are abiding in Christ, and vigilant and ruthless in dealing with sin as the Holy Spirit reveals it to us, we will defeat it but for those who are spiritually weak or have issues such as those childhood wounds outlined above, sexual sin can easily take root and spread, to the detriment of the host.

- Once leprosy has a foothold it usually begins to attack the extremities, the areas that are least "warm." This is usually the fingers, ears, nose, and toes. It attacks the nerves and the skin in these areas, causing them to become desensitized and without feeling, numb. Sexual sin is about medicating our pain, getting a "high" from an orgasm. Without knowing it, we are trying to feel better by numbing the feelings we don't want to feel or deal with; stress, anger, loneliness, fear, and boredom among others. But here is where the devil gets us; by numbing the feelings we don't want to feel, we also unwittingly numb the feelings we do want to feel; love, joy, peace, patience, gentleness etc. as well as numbing our receptivity to God, thus becoming blind and deaf to wooing of the Holy Spirit.

Leprosy, as with sexual sin, takes root and gains a foothold. It progresses without being visible to most other people. We still look good on the outside. We're still able to seemingly function in our family and Church life, but slowly, it begins to consume our thought life and emotions, deforming our souls and numbing our spiritual sensitivity. As it progresses through each stage, it ever so quietly begins destroying our relationship with Jesus Christ, our marriages, our relationships with others and our very souls.

At some point, if we are God's prodigal, by His grace and love, we are brought to our senses. God will reveal to us that the enemy has taken, with our own consent, all that is of true value from our lives. We are confronted with the need for true repentance and humility.

The people now seeking freedom from this sin represent the tip of the iceberg. With statistics showing that 12-17 year old boys are currently the biggest users of porn and that 60% of men and 30% of women in the Church are already addicted to porn,[3] *there is a tsunami wave of addiction to sexual sin about to hit the Church, with devastating results.*

We need to be prepared to put aside our judgment and joyfully offer love, education and pathways of deliverance to the body of which we are a part. Sexual sin, in all its forms is a humungous, cancerous tumor in the body of the Church and a great threat to many being without "spot or wrinkle" before the return of Christ. We must prepare to address it now!

Chapter 3 | What's in a Tsunami?

"Get Real" Questions for discussion with other men:

Are you shocked at the statistics on porn addiction in the Church?

How applicable do you think the analogy of sin to leprosy is in today's culture?

How do you feel about 12-17 year old boys being the largest consumers of pornography?

What is the future of marriage relationships for your children who are either using pornography or may very well marry users of pornography?

How prepared is your Church to deal with this sin?

Chapter 4 | Did I just choose Eve?

"If we are not in control of our appetites, our appetites will control us"[1]

"What has been will be again, what has been done will be done again; there is nothing new under the sun." (Ecclesiastes 1:9)

As powerfully new and overwhelming as sexual sin seems, we are not dealing with a new weakness in man or a new tactic of our enemy. Our susceptibility to this particular type of sin has been around since the beginning of recorded history, and the Bible is filled with stories of sexual temptation, sin and subsequent consequences.

How did all this start and why are we (men in particular) so weak when it comes to sex? It all started in the Garden of Eden. The book of Genesis tells the story of creation and the fall of man. In chapter 2 God created Adam and then acknowledges that it is not good for man to be alone, so God creates a woman, Eve, to be Adam's companion.

She must have been a stunning beauty, an untainted woman perfect in every possible way, fresh from the mind of God Himself. Adam was surely impressed and he must have cherished her deeply, after all, she was the only one of her kind and made specifically for him. How could two human beings be more perfectly matched?

Just imagine the amazement and beauty of that moment when the two of them first saw each other. There was no lust, no desire to conquer, captivate or manipulate for sexual gain, no embarrassment, no awkwardness, *simply sheer awe*. I suspect they were speechless at the beauty of each other. I heard a preacher once say that he couldn't prove it but the first words out of Adam's mouth must have been a stunned "WHOA!" and Eve was called whoa-man ever after! (I know...bad joke.)

Soon after, in Genesis 3 we find the leader of the fallen angels, Lucifer, posing as an innocent creature over which God had given Adam dominion and authority. The disguised Lucifer strikes up a conversation, a dialogue with Eve in an attempt to confuse, tempt, twist, and ultimately control what God had created.

Why does Lucifer hate us so?

The question arises, why does Lucifer hate us so? Why are we caught in this battle for sexual purity and what part do our choices play in the bigger picture? What is it about us that he wants so badly to destroy? Why is his animosity and evil intent focused on us? I have a few suggestions on this matter.

1. God made man and woman in his image and placed them in charge of the whole earth. They had authority over all of creation.

"Let us make human beings in our image, to be like us. They will reign over the fish in the sea, the birds in the sky, the livestock, all the wild animals on the earth, and the small animals that scurry along the ground. So God created human beings in his own image. In the image of God He created *them;* male and female He created them." (Genesis 1:26, 27)

God created man and woman to reflect him and have a special and personal relationship with Him. He delegated authority over this world, under his ultimate authority to Adam.

"What is man that you are mindful of him, the son of man that you care for him? **You made him a *little lower than the heavenly beings*** and crowned him with glory and honor. You made him ruler over the works of your hands; you put everything under his feet" (Psalm 8: 4, 5)

"When you are precious to God, you become important to Satan"

~ *Ron Hall* ~

In Psalm 8, King David is expressing awe and amazement that WE are the crowning achievement of God's creation; that mankind, through Adam was given dominion of this world in submission to God.

2. As a representation and extension of God Himself, man and woman, when they come together, have the ability to *create LIFE, in his image*. We have the ability

to extend the crowning achievement of God's creation! It is a power the adversary does not have and he hates us for having this power to create life and mirror the image of God.

Every child that is born is a thorn in the side of our enemy because we are reproducing the image of God! This ability to re-create the image of God through a sexual union has been the focus of much of the enemy's attacks throughout history, not *only* because man and woman in union can re-create life, but because it is through this process of creation that the savior would come to earth and crush the head of Satan (Gen 3:15). By corrupting and perverting sex, the process by which we re-create the image of God, Lucifer seduces us into destroying our own souls and perverting the purpose of our creation.

3. The pure, holy relationship of Man and Woman in marriage is meant to be a representative picture of Christ and his love for his bride, the Church.

Just as Eve was taken out of Adam's side while he slept, you could say she was "birthed" out of Adam's side, (Gen 2:21-22) you could also say the Church was "birthed" when a spear was thrust into Jesus' side, confirming his death (while He was "asleep," a word used to describe death). The love, sacrifice, and lifelong commitment in the marriage relationship are to be a reflection of Christ's love, sacrifice and commitment to his bride, the Church. It is part of how we are to live out life, reflecting the image of God. As such, Lucifer seeks to destroy this picture along with the representation of

Christ's love for us. Like an angry ex-lover slashing, breaking and destroying the pictures of his former love in a fit of jealousy, Lucifer hates everything that reminds him of the goodness of God and his love for his bride.

Godly marriage and holy sexual intimacy are an affront to the god of this world, and he will do everything he can to pervert, destroy and break the bonds and representative covenant of marriage. He attacks from within and without, using any and all avenues at his disposal; activists groups, social pressure, television, movies, music, internet, government legislation, advertising in all its forms, fashion, romance novels, liberal psychology, and on and on. There is nothing that he will not use to destroy marriage and pervert God's original design for our sexuality. His desire is to twist God's creation. Sexual union with one mate for life, physically becoming one, as we are to be one with God spiritually, is an integral part of God's design for marriage. From the enemy's perspective it must be destroyed in any way possible.

Caught between God and Eve

Lucifer, disguised as a lowly creature who looked non-threatening and innocent in appearance, engages Eve. He begins asking questions, probing her intellectual perimeter in an attempt to look for a weakness, a place to be exploited for his diabolical purposes. The Bible isn't absolutely clear where Adam was during this process. Was he was standing nearby, passively listening to the conversation? Had he and Eve been separated? In my experience we are much more susceptible to sin and deception when distance, anger or separation of some kind has come between us and our mate.

At any rate, the Bible says that Eve was tempted, seeing that the fruit was *pleasing to the eye* and that it was *desirable for gaining wisdom*. She was *deceived* and ate the fruit. The Bible says she gave some to Adam and he ate as well.

Now, I would like to entertain for a moment what might have gone through Adam's mind throughout this process. Remember, although Adam was fresh off the press, this man was no dummy; innocent yes, as we might measure innocence, but I am certain that his intellectual powers would far surpass those of modern man.

God had told Adam that if they ate of the fruit they would surely die. Whatever actual steps led to Adam finding out what had happened, when Eve presented the fruit to him and he became aware of what she had done, he had to be conscious and mindful of the consequences God had stated regarding this disobedience.

He must have thought something along the lines of ..."You ate the fruit and you aren't dead? The serpent said you wouldn't die and you are still alive. God said you would die and you didn't....did God mean what he said? Did He lie to us? Did I misunderstand?" The enemy had succeeded in one of his favorite ploys, creating confusion; a confusion that surely caused Adam to begin to question the truthfulness of what God had told him.

When confusion is present, the scale of our willpower will tip in the direction of what our flesh desires. It is not possible to have sin-resisting faith when we are confused or doubt the word of God. When we are unsure about the consequences of sin due to uncertainty or doubt, we have entered the enemy's camp. This is where the desires of our heart have the power to manipulate our intellect. Our decieved intellect will direct our will. That is why we MUST know the word of God and have a personal faith in its trustworthiness. The word of God is a bridle on the desires of the human heart.

"One of Satan's most deceptive and powerful ways of defeating us is to get us to believe a lie. And the biggest lie is that there are no consequences to our own doing. Satan will give you whatever you ask if it will lead you to where he ultimately wants you"

~ Charles Stanley ~

Adam now had a choice before him. Would he believe and trust God *contrary to what his intellect and senses were telling him* or would he choose to join Eve, this woman that he loved, this perfect mate and ...the only one of her kind, in her sin?

If Adam chose to believe God, he may have considered that Eve would die for her sin just as God had said. If this were to happen, then he would be left alone. He would be without this beautiful female creation made specifically for him. She was the only human companion and love he had ever known. Even if God made him another, how could she replace the memory of his beautiful Eve? Their hearts were knit together in a first love I don't think we can possibly comprehend. They were one flesh in the first and purest, most innocent and intimate marriage covenant.

His heart must have been deeply torn, his mind racing. If he chose to join her in sin maybe, *just maybe* they could remain together. After all she wasn't dead, and she had eaten the fruit, right? Maybe God hadn't been telling the truth. Or maybe he hadn't understood God correctly? Or maybe there was a way around the consequences that God had decreed?

Eve was deceived into sin by Lucifer directly, but Lucifer succeeded in putting Adam in a place where he was *forced* to choose between God and something he dearly loved and treasured. I have no doubt that Adam felt he needed and couldn't live without his precious Eve. Adam's sin was by choice, his eyes open. He was not deceived.

It was a masterful chess move by the enemy. The Bible in its succinctness makes it seem like Eve offered the fruit and Adam blindly and immediately took it and ate. But I prefer to think that Adam was tortured in his decision. How else could God hold him accountable? I believe he suffered under this temptation to choose between his love for God and his love for Eve. Why had she put him in this position? Knowing that he had to choose between God his creator and his wife, must have been a terrible gut-wrenching dilemma for Adam.

In the end, Adam chose Eve, the love and physical, tangible comfort offered by a woman over trusting God. Adam's sin is very nearly the same as ours. He chose to meet his need for companionship and comfort by choosing Eve over trusting and choosing to believe what God had said to him, just as we often choose the shortcut offered by the very same enemy that deceived the parents of our race. Apparently, the genetic apple doesn't fall far from the tree.

Chapter 4 | Did I just choose Eve?

"Get Real" Questions for discussion with other men:

Can you explain what Satan hopes to accomplish in his attack on sexual union? Does this make sense to you?

Does it change your view of the consequences of sexual sin i.e. adultery, divorce, abortion, children shuttled between homes, missing fathers?

Why do you think God held Adam and not Eve responsible for the sin in the garden?

Can you relate to Adam's struggle between choosing Eve or God? In what way?

How do you feel about the reality that when we choose pornography we are choosing sexual comfort over God?

Authors note: Please consider providing a review of The Purity Driven Life on Amazon.com.

Chapter 5 | Worship What?

"Most of us spend the first six days of the week sowing wild oats; then go to Church on Sunday and pray for a crop failure"[1]

"Do not be deceived, **God will not be mocked;** *for whatever a man sows, this he will also reap."* (Galatians 6:7)

You probably think of idolatry as bowing down and worshipping images of wood and stone or maybe a golden calf. However, idolatry goes far beyond that. We become idolaters when we allow some idea, some place, some thing, some desire or some person to become more important to us than our Savior. When we choose *anything* over God, we commit idolatry. The Bible is filled with admonishments against this sin.

In modern America we mentally recoil at the idea of worshiping wood and stone idols. However, our lives and society are filled with idols. We have all seen film of fans as the Beatles, Michael Jackson, Lady Gaga or the latest super celebrity make an appearance. People are screaming, crying, hands raised waving desperately, wanting to just get a touch, an autograph, or some type of acknowledgment of their loyalty and adoration for their beloved. We would say these are extreme fans but whether they acknowledge it or not, they are engaged in worship in the truest sense of the word.

I know I am about to poke a very sensitive spot, but what about sports fans? As I write this the Super Bowl is about to start. Some fans cheer, scream, paint their faces and even fight in defense of their teams. Isn't that why a man would wear a shirt with the name of another man on his back, as a form of expressing a desire to be like his idol? In Texas, even local high school football games are almost given a sacred status. If you doubt me, try criticizing the football team and see what happens. There are frequently riots around the world after championship soccer matches. These are all forms of idolatry.

The world's marketing executives are constantly seeking new ways to exploit each new wave of fan worship, selling all kinds of paraphernalia capitalizing on the trend. Each year the t-shirts, caps and other clothing are redesigned in order to get the fans coming back and giving yearly "offerings" to their team. We have a show called "American Idol" and there is even a condition called "Celebrity Worship Syndrome." In summarizing the results of a recent study of approximately, 700 people aged 18 to 60; I found the following quote,

"One in three people (33%) are so obsessed with someone in the public eye that he or she is a *sufferer* say psychologists. And one in four is so taken with their idol that the obsession affects their daily life."[2]

This book is about sexual sin, and in that context let's talk about sex as a form of idol worship. According to the statistics quoted previously, 60% of all men sitting in Church regularly worship via immoral sex in its many forms and perversions. To do so is to choose sexual sin over God.

If you are a Christian, you might be thinking, "I love God. I don't *choose* sexual sin over God, I just can't stop. It's not that bad, who am I hurting? We're just being guys, right?" Let me ask you a question, if your wife is having an affair with her boss and you find out, how comforting it is for her to say "but... I really do love you! I just can't say no to him! My heart is yours but my body just can't resist him!"

> *"An Idol of the mind is as offensive to God as an idol of the hand."*
>
> ~ A.W. Tozer ~

God see's your sin, there is no hiding it. He knows what you are doing, and if you are a Christian who is filled with the Holy Spirit, by choosing to give in to your own lust and desire you are forcing the Holy Spirit to participate in your sin with you. I know I've said this more than once, but it is a sobering reality that I want you to remember. Jesus in speaking of Holy Spirit that lives in us said,

"And I will ask the Father, and He will give you another Helper, to be with you forever." (John 14:16)

Everywhere you go, everything you do, God the Holy Spirit is with you, even when we choose to worship the idols of this age. This pure and sinless member of the trinity is willing to live in a defiled temple in order to help you get victory over your sin. That is how much God loves you! As Christian men, we need to get real and honest about our actions and the choices we make.

When I used to sit and look at a beautiful woman on my screen, I would think thoughts like; "That is AWEsome. That is beautiful. That is unbelievable. That is amazing. I need a woman like that. Life would be perfect if I had someone like her."

I was giving these images (and the demonic forces behind them) my praise and adoration. In the clarity of sobriety, I now recognize these thoughts as nothing but worship and idolatry, and it truly breaks my heart when I think of how unfaithful I was. I was engaged in objectifying and worshiping these beautiful women. Like a "fish on the line" I could fight it for a while, but then the devil would just let out a little line until I was weakened by fatigue, anger, bitterness, jealousy, or just opportunity, and then he would reel me in again and repeat the process until I was caught up in his net. I bet you can relate, and I hope you are seeing the reality of the idolatry in sexual sin.

Humility...or humiliation

If you have read this far and are engaged in sexual sin, you realize you are deeply broken and sinful, and probably deeply ashamed. Hopefully, you are broken enough to admit your inability to control your participation in sexual sin. Maybe you bought this book because you have been caught and are desperately looking for answers. I heard a preacher once say, "God's plan for his children is either humility or humiliation, and you get to choose." If you are feeling humiliation as a consequence of your sin, God finally has your attention.

Statistics show that *91% of the men seeking help by joining a men's accountability group do so only because they were busted* by their wife and given an ultimatum.[3] That means only a paltry 9% had the character to step up, conquer their pride and be obedient to God on their own without being externally pressed to do so. Only 9% voluntarily walk out James 5:16 without God having to use their wife or some other circumstances to "encourage" them into dealing with their sin.

Lest you feel condemned by that last paragraph, I am sad to say I have to include myself in the 91%. In my pride, I wanted to avoid appearing weak before others. I didn't want to admit I couldn't deal with my struggles on my own. I wanted to appear in control of myself. My pride was more important to me than confronting my sin, even when I knew it was wrong. I didn't want to humble myself before others and admit my weakness. But God in his unconditional love provided a way to humble me! I am so grateful that he loves me that much! God was much more concerned about the condition of my heart than my comfort or what others would think of me.

Selling your soul for a crappy meal

The bondage and deceitfulness of sexual sin is so powerful and alluring. Most Christian men will choose to pridefully struggle quietly on their own until they get caught, or die trying to keep this sin hidden. The very heart-wrenching sadness is that God has a destiny for each and every man to be a warrior for Him. To be taking ground for His kingdom alongside his brothers in Christ and teaching his children to continue the battle after he has gone to heaven. However, a man who harbors sexual sin will eventually be turned over to the control of his ungodly desires (Romans 1:28). He will eventually be unable to hear God's voice or sense the conviction of the Holy Spirit. It will be nothing but a faint whisper, causing him to wonder if he is imagining things. His choices put him at risk of forfeiting his destiny and calling.

Hebrews 12 is great chapter to read if you want to learn about the seriousness of sexual sin. Look at what God says through the writer, starting with verse 14.

"Make every effort to live in peace with everyone and to be holy; without holiness no one will see the Lord....See that no one is sexually immoral, or is godless like Esau, who for a single meal sold his inheritance rights as the oldest son. Afterward, as you know, when he wanted to inherit this blessing, he was rejected. Even though he sought the blessing with tears, he could not change what he had done."

> "God can never entrust... anyone who has not been broken of pride, for pride is the armor of darkness itself."
>
> ~ Francis Frangipane ~

When Satan tempts us and we *choose* inappropriate sexual fulfillment over obedience to God's plan for us, the writer equates it to selling our inheritance for a single meal (truly junk food). A solitary moment of sexual pleasure is delightful to the senses but has no lasting satisfaction. Rather, it is spiritually destructive. In fact, we will want more in just a few hours. It is almost as if we have a spiritual tapeworm that prevents us from obtaining proper nutrition, regardless of how much we eat. There is no amount of consumption or participation that will or can bring lasting satisfaction. The hunger will return. In contrast Jesus says in Matthew 5:6,

"Blessed are those who **hunger and thirst for righteousness**, for they will be *filled*."

The hunger for righteousness is the natural state of a man filled with the Spitit of God. Tony Evans makes the following point on this subject.

"When visiting the doctor's office the doctor will often inquire about your appetite. A lack of physical appetite is a symptom of physical illness. A lack of appetite for God's word and presence is a symptom of spiritual disease. If we are physically hungry we will do whatever is necessary to get some type of food for our bodies yet we often allow our spirit to go days, weeks or months without spiritual food."[4]

It is interesting to note that the same fleshly desires related to the lust of the eyes and our appetite for food is what started this whole thing in the garden. If we refuse to yield our appetites to God and submit our ungodly appetites to Him, our appetites in all their various forms will control us, and potentially our eternal destiny.

If you are ready to admit you have been engaged in sexual idolatry, or if you have been caught and are dealing with this sin, I suggest you immediately get on your knees and thank God. Thank Him that he loves you enough to humble you and get your attention. If you haven't been caught...yet, I urge you to set your pride aside and *run* to Jesus and the resources of the local Church or local ministries to get some love and help.

The stakes are too high, and you cannot win this battle in isolation. The temptation to believe that you can deal with this on your own is a powerful, pride-filled lie of the enemy. I look back on the painful process of deliverance from sexual sin, ultimately at the cost of humiliation before friends, family, co-workers and my Church, the loss of my in-laws' respect, the loss of my marriage, as worth it all in order to be able to stand before my Savior as clean vessel, fit for the Master's use.

The Seeds of our Destruction

Ralph Waldo Emerson is known to have said, "Sow a thought and you reap an action; sow an act and you reap a habit; sow a habit and you reap a character; sow a character and you reap a destiny."

Actually, God said it first through the Apostle Paul:

"Do not be deceived, **God will not be mocked;** for whatever a man sows, this he will also reap." (Galatians 6:7)

You should view this verse as a promise from the God of the universe that you cannot and will not escape the consequences of sexual sin. Allowing us to escape our harvest would be a mockery against God and violate a key spiritual law. Reaping what we sow implies a harvest, and every harvest requires planting seeds. Just as in the natural world, the spiritual world operates on this same foundational principle. The verse that follows Galatians 6:7 says:

"Whoever sows to *please their flesh,* from the flesh will reap destruction; whoever sows to *please the Spirit,* from the Spirit will reap eternal life."

Just as Satan appeared to Eve as a simple, lowly non-threatening creature, sexual sin always starts with those little, seemingly innocent sexual thoughts that we allow to take root in our mind. Paul exhorts us in 2 Corinthians 10:5 to:

"Take every thought captive to obey Christ."

Christ Himself tells us that:

"Everyone who looks at a woman with *lustful intent* has already committed adultery with her in his heart." (Matthew 5:28)

Impure sexual thoughts allowed to take up residency in our mind become fantasies, fantasy leads to desire. Then this desire will transform itself by the consummation of sexual action. Sexual action leads to addiction of the fantasy process, which in turn leads to a destiny defined by the consequences of sin. The fallout from sexual addiction is; adultery, sexual diseases, aborted babies, failed marriages, divorce, broken children and in addition, potentially eternal consequences. The children of the sexual addict become forced to participate in suffering the repercussions of a father's sin that began with selfish desire. It all starts so "innocently." James, the brother of Jesus says it this way.

"...but each person is tempted when they are dragged away by their own evil desire and enticed. Then after desire has conceived, it gives birth to sin, and sin, when it is full-grown, gives birth to death." (James 1:14, 15)

First Exposure

In all the men's groups I have been in there are certain themes that come up regularly. Most of the men were exposed to porn between 8 and 12 years old. Often they found their dad's "stash" or a magazine discarded in the woods, in the trash, or at a neighbor's house. Today, most 8-12 year olds are finding sexual content far more readily, on the Internet or via smart phone.

This first exposure experience is so common that we often joke that we are all finding the same magazines. The devil just keeps recycling them and placing them where young boys are sure to find them! The men will often talk about how powerful this first exposure was imprinted on their soul. My first exposure was about the age of twelve. I still vividly remember to this day, almost 40 years later, the sexual cartoon that caught my attention, the sexual acts portrayed, and how excited I felt when I saw it.

Many men talk of the eyes of the beautiful woman they saw in that first magazine and how inviting and accepting they were. There was no rejection, only a feeling of absolute acceptance, safety, and excitement. You see, at its roots, pornography and sexual sin are not about sex. They are about the God shaped hole in our hearts. Long before Hugh Hefner or the internet, G.K. Chesterton was quoted as saying,

"Every man who knocks on the door of a brothel is looking for God."

Although all of our stories are similar, each is also different and unique. The building blocks that make up the foundation of our individual weaknesses to the various types of sexual sin are an interwoven maze. Our Individual sexual templates are a labyrinth of the wounds that life has inflicted on us and our partially effective attempts to control our circumstances, pain and emotions.

In looking back on my life, I now see clearly the circumstances and events that shaped my behavior and caused my particular weakness in this area. I can also see how the enemy was deliberate in planting those seeds, nurturing, and cultivating the weakness of my early life. He was patiently waiting to reap his harvest until the maximum damage could be sustained. This seems to be a favorite tactic of his.

Dead men walking

How many pastors only get caught after they have huge ministries, often with a worldwide following? The twentieth century is riddled with debris from fallen pastors; in fact, news broke just yesterday of another man who pastors a 20,000 member Church caught in adultery. This stumbling doesn't "just happen." The seeds of sexual sin in these leaders lie hidden (from the perspective of the outside observer) until exposure will cause the most harm to the Church. I immediately think of Jim Bakker, Jimmy Swaggart, Ted Haggard, Bob Gray, and so many others that have fallen and brought the world's mockery upon Jesus and His Church. It happens every day on a smaller scale as families are destroyed by the sinful choices of husbands and fathers.

When we won't voluntarily humble ourselves before God and deal radically with our sin, we live on the devil's timetable. When we refuse to get clean with God and deal decisively with our sin, it is like allowing the devil to maintain a suicide bomb in our heart and soul that he controls with a suicide switch. He waits for the opportune time to activate the explosion for maximum destructive effect, on his schedule and at his will.

When you willingly sin, you are his to devour. (1 Peter 5:8) You are his slave. (John 8:34) When he whistles, you come running. Unless you truly repent and get serious about your sin, this scenario will continue. Often it will only end when you are caught and lose everything or are threatened with the loss of everything. Sometimes even then, we are unwilling to give up our sin and choose God's way. Sometimes it's just too late, our hearts have hardened.

As long as our pride causes us to think we can or must deal with this in our own power, we will continue to attempt to "manage" our sin. It is in this place that we justify our actions and slowly become blind to the reality of what is happening as the sin slowly but surely takes more and more territory in our mind and soul. Our Enemy patiently squeezes out of our life the ability to maintain our relationship with God, and ultimately all other healthy relationships.

So many Christian men give up and just concede that this sin is like an "itch" that has to be scratched every so often just to experience a modicum of peace. We justify our behavior by blaming our wives or claiming "I'm just a man; this is how we are...after all that is what grace is for!" Oh how we misunderstand grace. It must cause Christ great pain to watch us wallow in our sin, ignorant of the deliverance He has bought for us at such great cost to Himself.

If you haven't given up and have been trying to win this battle on your own, then you know it's like trying to bail water out of a boat with a hole in the hull. The devil makes sure that the hole is just big enough that although your boat is filling with water, it is slow enough that you think you have the problem under control. The ship is slowly sinking, but your best hope, from the perspective of prideful thinking, is to keep bailing and hope that you can stay afloat.

Our enemy has been around since before the beginning of this world. He is more intelligent than you and I. He has thousands of years of experience in deceiving, enslaving and torturing mankind. He is so crafty that he is even willing to let you think you have this sin under control for periods of time. He wants you to become confident, complacent and proud in your own ability, and then... when you are least expecting it, he provides a temptation you can't resist and you bow down once again in worshipful obedience.

Chapter 5 | Worship What?

"Get Real" Questions for discussion with other men:

How do you feel about the idea of God allowing us to be humiliated and exposed because He loves us?

Can you relate to men not dealing with this sin until they are found out? In what way?

Are you able to look back and see how the bad "seeds" that nurtured your weakness for sexual sin were planted in your life? How did you contribute to their growth?

How do you feel about the idea of the enemy wanting to "blow up" your life in such a way as to achieve maximum destruction? How will he do it?

Chapter 6 | Programmed to Salivate

"Garbage in, garbage out"[1]....You are what you eat"[2]

"As a man thinks in his heart so is he." (Proverbs 23:7)

"Those who make idols are like them; so is everyone who trusts in and relies on them." (Psalm 135:18)

When I was in my teens, my family went to visit my relatives in the deep backwoods of Tennessee. If you haven't been to Tennessee let me tell you, the food is amazing and the accents are as thick as the molasses baked beans! Half the time I couldn't understand what was being said so I just kept eating. After only one short week, I noticed an interesting thing. Without even realizing what was happening, I started to talk with a Tennessee accent! (Oh, and I gained a pound a day!)

I find it interesting that God created us as naturally wired to be influenced, to emulate something or someone. We have an innate bent to worship. Our behavior and our desires are shaped and fueled by what holds our focus and by those people and things we surround and associate ourselves with. Paul states,

"Do not be misled: Bad company corrupts good character." (1 Corinthians 15:33)

Conversely, the wise King Solomon said,

"Walk with the wise and become wise." (Proverbs 13:20)

This same idea is precisely why advertisers use sex to get our focus and attention, because it works, even to sell coffee. In 2003, the first Cowgirls espresso opened in the heart of Washington State, the birthplace of Starbucks. You would think that any entrepreneur with a coffee bean of wisdom would not want to go head to head with the most successful retail coffee establishment in history. However, Cowgirls had a secret weapon more powerful than the addictive power of caffeine. The concept was scantily clad, beautiful young women in bikinis stooping to serve you coffee at the drive up window. Their stores often have long lines of (mostly) men waiting to get a peek. They are so popular that they have grown to 13 locations and are now franchising.[3]

Sexual arousal, and I am referring to just the seeing, or thinking of sexually related content (such as seeing scantily clad women serving us coffee), changes the way we process information and make decisions. The response of the male mind to seeing something sexual is not unlike that of Pavlov's dog. Pavlov is the Russian Physiologist primarily known for his work related to classical conditioning. Pavlov would ring a bell every time he served a dog its dinner and it wasn't long before he could just ring the bell and the dog would begin to involuntarily salivate.[4]

Getting our bell rung

A dog's hunger and desire for tasty food is completely natural, and when seeing food, it is natural for him to salivate in anticipation of eating it. What Pavlov discovered is that if the bell is rung consistently when the dog is served food, the dog begins to associate the natural desire for food with the ringing of the bell. It wasn't long before the bell by itself was enough to elicit the salivation response.

> "... the safest road to Hell is the gradual one-the gentle slope, soft underfoot, without sudden turnings, without milestones, without signposts."
>
> ~ C.S. Lewis ~

This is precisely what advertisers are attempting to do to you; associate your natural "hunger," desires and feelings about sex with their product, and it works! Why else would they be willing to pay millions of dollars to reach you by having beautiful babes seductively eating their brand of burger, chips or beer? I hope you get the idea...the list of examples is nearly endless.

The devil works in the same way. He seeks to establish a connection in us to where all he has to do is "ring the bell" and we involuntarily "salivate" for the sin he offers. Being wired with a fleshly nature that desires and is attracted to sexual sin is a fact in all of us. The devil knows this and his pattern is to exploit this weakness in such a way that we not only lose the ability to control it, we don't even understand how or why we are unable to resist the pull.

We are all born with this sin nature, and it is for our deliverance that God came to empower us, to put our sin nature in subjection. It is a fact that we become increasingly like what we worship, and it is in choosing who (or what) we will worship that our dominion over sin, or sin's dominion over us is determined.

Becoming programmed

So how does this process of becoming "Pavlov's dog" take place within us? There are certain broad yet predictable categories in the progression of sexual sin. I once heard a preacher categorize them according to the effort required to engage in them.

They all merge together in their damage to the soul, but some are more difficult to see and deal with from a human perspective, particularly in the early stages. I think it helpful to review these. He categorized them as 1) No effort sexual sin, 2) Low effort sexual sin and 3) High effort sexual sin.

The seeds of sin are planted with no effort sin and naturally progress toward high effort sin. [5]

1. No effort sin would be those thoughts and fantasies you have in your head, your thought life. They require no effort to access, and in fact, once you begin to allow your mind to feed in this way, it will not be long before these types of thoughts begin to breed. Once they start to reproduce, it is almost impossible to keep them at bay. They begin to consume your thought life and displace

the pure thoughts you used to have; changing the way you see the world, women and sexuality. These thoughts can even become a form of torture because you cannot keep them out of your mind. Before long, they are bombarding you from every direction whether you want them or not, they begin to control your thinking. Ephesians 6:16 speaks of the fiery darts of the enemy where we are told to...

"...take up the shield of faith, with which you can extinguish all the flaming arrows of the evil one."

This brings to my mind the scene from old cowboy movies where flaming arrows are shot at a building or covered wagon in an attempt to force the hero out into the open for the kill shot. These fiery darts are delivered from every direction to set your "house" on fire in an effort to entice you from your safe room of abiding in Christ. It is impossible to quench or extinguish these thoughts without the power of the Holy Spirit, faith and a renewed mind.

2. An example of low effort sin would be an interaction with internet porn. It doesn't necessarily require advance planning. You might be working on an assignment after everyone has gone to bed and up pops a risqué picture. Then in two or three clicks you have opened the door to sin. Little or no forethought and planning were required, but once it presents itself you are caught.

3. High effort sexual sin would be defined as those sins that require greater effort in thought and planning to commit. A sexual affair would be an example. An affair

requires forethought, fantasy, flirting, an approach, emotional engagement, a liaison and ultimately, maybe an ongoing secret relationship which requires a planned cover-up and lying about behavior and whereabouts.

Here is what is interesting about each of these categories. Sexual sin starts with the no effort sins of the thought life and progresses to low effort. If the battle to extinguish sin isn't engaged aggressively during the early stages of these "little things," the sin can grow and weave its wicked tentacles throughout your life until it becomes a stronghold in your life escalating toward high effort sins. As sexual sin escalates from no effort to low effort to high effort, the sin, thank God, becomes increasingly difficult to hide. When discovered, the sinner will either choose to continue the behavior despite the consequences or begin to take the steps needed to repent and surrender this sinful behavior to God.

"The essence of temptation is the invitation to live independently of God."

~ Neil T. Anderson ~

The Prodigal

Jesus tells the story in Luke 15:11-32 of a father with two sons living in his house. The younger is enticed by the promise of all that the world offers, what looks to be a life of easy everything, easy money, easy popularity, easy acclaim and easy love. The son takes all that the father has given him and leaves home to chase after all that the world offers.

For a season he thinks that he has found true happiness, the cure for all that causes him pain and anguish, but inevitably and eventually he loses everything and the pleasures of the world no longer cover his pain or drown the hunger in his soul. Like all pleasurable sin, the more he gets, the more he thinks he wants and needs. In the end, the consequences of his choices lead him to see he is emptier and hungrier than he ever was.

There comes a point where he realizes all these things he is chasing will never provide lasting satisfaction, they are ultimately empty. In fact, his eyes are opened. He comes to know the truth of his situation and realizes that his pursuit has been a mistake, a detour of futility. And so, empty-handed and barren of anything to offer his father, he decides to return to his father's house in humility… and humiliation.

And, here is the most beautiful part. As he returns with nothing to offer, broken and humbled, he finds that his father has been waiting, looking for the prodigal to return home every day since he chose to leave. He realizes that his father's love is desirable, not for what the father can give him or provide for him, but because the father loves him with a pure and true love beyond what he can comprehend. The prodigal realizes his father longs desperately to be in a relationship with him. This love is not based on what he can offer his father or what gifts or talents he brings to the relationship. He learns his father loves him simply because of who he is, the child of the father.

It is out of God's compassion that, when we choose to continually embrace sin He allows our sin to eventually consume our life. It is His grace that allows us to come to the broken place where we voluntarily admit our emptiness, our helplessness, and turn to Him in humility. If we refuse to humble ourselves, it is also His grace that allows our sin to be revealed, and we suffer the humiliation of exposure. Sometimes, being laid bare before all that we hold dear is the most loving thing God can do to get our attention. Hebrews 12:3-17 says,

"God disciplines those He loves."

Like any good father He warns us about the consequences of sexual sin and begs us to trust Him and follow the path He has laid out for us. He promises,

"...no good thing will be withheld from those who do what is right" (Psalm 84:11)

But, like every father-child relationship, there comes a time when the father allows the child to experience the consequences of choices insisted upon.

Boys will be boys

In many situations where a man is bondage to this sin, the wife is aware of what is happening. Our wives are often more sensitive than we are spiritually, but out of embarrassment and fear she doesn't want anyone to find out about her husband's sin. She may feel his addiction is a confirmation that something is wrong with her. She may feel that if she were thinner or more beautiful or younger, then her husband wouldn't "need" something besides her, so she tries to ignore the problem. She suffers in her own way because of your sin, until she says "enough!" and either leaves or gives the ultimatum.

We are taught by television, music, music videos, commercials, celebrities and culture in general from infancy that boys will be boys. They will sow their wild oats and mark their manhood by sexual exploration and conquest. We are deceived into thinking we can sow these seeds without reaping a harvest. We often think that once we find that one special girl and marry her all those desires will miraculously go away. If you are married, isn't that what you thought? How many men prior to marriage thought, "Once I get married I will no longer lust for other women because *then* I will be getting all the sex I want and need?" That is the deceitfulness of sin.

If you have been married long you laugh at this because you know this is a lie from the pit of hell. Up until marriage most men have spent their entire life letting sexual fantasies run wild, at least to some extent, thinking that marriage is the cure. Indeed, doesn't the bible seem to suggest this when Paul said "if they cannot control themselves let them marry: for it is better to marry than to burn" (1 Corinthians 7:9). Our thought life doesn't automatically transform into that of a loving, dutiful, godly husband just because we get married. And when our lusts don't disappear after marriage, the evolution of the lie begins to tell you that you married the wrong woman. The devil is a master at keeping us focused in the wrong direction. "Lord it's not my fault; it's the woman you gave me."

To determine the real issue we have to look inward at the selfishness of our own hearts. The most difficult of sins to deal with are the idols related to the thought life, the no effort sexual sins, and this is where the battle must end if you ever hope to have lasting victory.

Most men don't realize that the devil has been programming them by ringing the bell of their thought life for years. It isn't until they try to take control of their thoughts that they begin to realize they have been programmed to "salivate" on command whenever the devil shoots a flaming arrow their way. They have become increasingly filled with lust, just like the idols they worship. (Psalm 135:15-18; Genesis 6:5)

Chapter 6 | Programmed to salivate

"Get Real" Questions for discussion with other men:

Can you see the progression of sexual sin in your life, starting with seemingly innocent thoughts?

Who told you these "thoughts" were OK?

Can you relate to enemy's' attacks as thoughts sent to enflame you?

Can you relate to being "tortured" or "bombarded" with lustful thoughts?

How do you feel about the father in the story of the prodigal waiting every day, looking for his son to return as a picture of God waiting for you?

Did you think that "lust" would disappear when you got married?

Chapter 7 | Shadows of Freedom

"Some often repent, yet never reform; they resemble a man traveling in a dangerous path, who frequently starts and stops, but never turns back."[1]

"Remember that for 40 years the LORD your God led you on your journey in the desert. He did this in order to humble you and test you. He wanted to know whether or not you would wholeheartedly obey his commands." (Deuteronomy 8:2)

In speaking about the Old Testament, Paul tell us,

"Now all these things happened unto them by way of example, (as a type or pattern) and are written for our admonition (authoritative counsel or warning), upon whom the ends of the world are come." (1 Corinthians 10:11)

Paul tells us that the books documenting the history of the Exodus and entry into the Promised Land are not just a historical record; they are also intended to be examples for us to learn from. They reveal a pattern by which we can see how we are to be led by Christ into the Spirit-filled life. They also reveal warnings regarding the consequences of refusing to obey God's laws.

In looking at God's relationship to his holy people, we see God deliver them from Pharaoh in order to become his nation of chosen people. The narrative of this deliverance is found in the book of Exodus. The Israelites' contribute *nothing* to their opportunity to be free from Pharaoh. It was all God's doing. He initiated it, He orchestrated it and He brought it to pass. God hardened Pharaoh's heart to ensure the Israelites' living conditions were so uncomfortable that they were ready to leave the life of slavery behind. When Moses said "let's go!" they were ready and willing to move.

In Joyous celebration, they took their families and all their belongings and followed Moses on a journey that would lead them to a Promised Land. They were only six days out of Egypt when the first test of their faith in God was presented. When they came to the Red Sea, Moses received the following instructions from the Lord.

"Tell the Israelites to turn back and encamp near Pi Hahiroth, between Migdol and the sea. They are to encamp by the sea, directly opposite Baal Zephon. Pharaoh will think, 'The Israelites are wandering around the land in confusion, hemmed in by the desert.' And *I will harden Pharaoh's heart, and he will pursue them*. But I will gain glory for myself through Pharaoh and all his army, and the Egyptians will know that I am the LORD." So the Israelites did this." (Exodus 14:1-4)

God had the nation's destiny completely under control. He was orchestrating this event to reveal himself to his people and the Egyptians. However when the Israelites saw Pharaoh and his army marching after them to take them back into slavery or kill them if they resisted, they panicked in fear!

If you look at a map of the Exodus, God had led them into a position where there was nowhere to run. Israel was an infant nation, untrained in battle. They had women and children among them. From an earthly perspective there would be nothing to do but submit to whatever Pharaoh was about to do to them. They were helpless, and they literally freaked out!

However, God had a plan. He was trying to teach his children to trust him. He wasn't about to let them be destroyed and placed a pillar of fire between the Israelites and the Egyptian army to protect his people. He supernaturally stepped in to protect his infant nation until He provided a way of deliverance. In the natural, there seemed no way of escape; however, God provided a miracle, one they never anticipated, the parting of the Red Sea. Moses led the nation through the sea safely to other side and God drowned the Egyptian Army who pursued them.

For those who become New Testament believers, God allows us to sense the misery of our condition and romances us out the "world." He causes us to hunger for that which is spiritual. However our enemy pursues us and will not let us go easily. Just as the nation of Israel did nothing to earn their freedom other than following the leading of Moses, we cannot earn this initial deliverance from our bondage to the god of this world. We have only to accept the offer of the journey toward the promise and choose to participate in the process. The Israelites' life and future prior to their deliverance from Egypt was one of unending slavery and bondage to the bidding of the slave master. So is the life of a man before accepting Christ as his deliverer.

> *"There is no circumstance, no trouble, no testing, that can ever touch me until, first of all it has gone...past Christ, right through to me. If it has come that far it has come with a great purpose, which I may not understand at the moment."*
>
> ~Alan Redpath ~

The exit (salvation) from Egypt and the journey into the desert wilderness was not the entry into the Promised Land. Likewise, our salvation is just the beginning of our journey with Christ. The desert wilderness was a place of testing and growth. When we first come to Christ, it takes all the faith we have to believe the simplicity of the Gospel and comprehend the spiritual reality of the gift of salvation that Christ has for each of us individually.

A symbol of Baptism

In the wilderness where God leads us, the opportunity to trust God at his word is tested and disobedience and sin are meant to be purged. The wilderness is where faith has the opportunity to take root and grow, while plucking up the weeds of sin. In this process, we begin to develop spiritual character and a heart willingness to trust Christ at his word. We are taught to act in obedience to him rather than lean on our own logic and reasoning. (2 Corinthians 10:5)

Paul teaches that the Israelites passing through the Red Sea is a shadow or type of the New Testament believer's baptism in water.

"For I do not want you to be ignorant of the fact, brothers and sisters, that our ancestors were all under the cloud and that they all passed through the sea. They were all baptized into Moses in the cloud and in the sea. They all ate the same spiritual food and drank the same spiritual drink; for they drank from the spiritual rock that accompanied them, and that rock was Christ." (1 Corinthians 10:1-4)

Just as the Israelites were baptized into and under the authority of Moses, the New Testament believer is baptized into and under the authority of Jesus and into the body of Christ, the Church. This baptism is meant to be a marker indicating that we are set free from the authority of the worldly slave master. Paul describes it this way.

"Shall we go on sinning so that grace may increase? By no means! We died to sin; how can we live in it any longer? Or don't you know that all of us who were baptized into Christ Jesus were baptized into his death? We were therefore buried with him through baptism into death in order that, just as Christ was raised from the dead through the glory of the Father, we too may live a new life." (Romans 6:2-4)

Our water baptism is to be a physical representation of what happened to us spiritually. The old, sinful man has died with Christ. (We descend into the water just as a Christ was put in the earth) and we are raised again, born afresh to a new life produced by and in connection to the power of God in us. Baptism is a picture of our spiritual connection to God being restored and our being raised to new life.

Many believers stop here, however this is not what God intended for us. It is the beginning of a relationship with God where we are tested with the goal of reaching a spiritual maturity and bearing the fruit of the Spirit. Even in our natural world, growth in our maturity is measured by instruction and testing.

Our teachers give us lessons to learn and then test us to ensure we have mastered the material. Entering school is not the end, the destination. It is the beginning of the learning and growing process. If we fail to learn those early lessons, we do not pass to the next stage and must repeat the work until we have learned the lesson. So it is with spiritual maturity. We don't get seniority for time served.

Seeking old comforts

After God's deliverance through the Red Sea and the destruction of the Egyptians, Moses leads the people to Mount Sinai where they set up camp. They have been out of Egypt about 60 days when Moses ascends the mountain to meet with God where he will be given the Ten Commandments. In their impatience, the people grow weary of waiting for Moses (and God) and seek comfort and entertainment by returning to the ways they had left behind. They plan a party around an idol fashioned in the image of a golden calf, which was one of the chief gods of Egypt.

> "The Bible recognizes no faith that does not lead to obedience, nor does it recognize any obedience that does not spring from faith. The two are at opposite sides of the same coin."
>
> ~ A. W. Tozer, ~

We are tempted to do the very same thing. When we don't sense God's presence, or feel that God isn't hearing us, or feel He isn't leading in the way we think He should, our inclination is to retreat to our old sinful behaviors. We easily fall back into old familiar, carnal patterns because our trust and faith in his promises are not sufficiently developed.

So God deals with the sin of their idolatry, gives them the Ten Commandments and they remain camped at Sinai for about eleven more months. God then instructs Moses to begin moving them toward the land of promise, and approximately two years after leaving Egypt, they arrive at Kadesh Barnea.

Kadesh Barnea was a place of major testing that would determine the course of their lives. It was here that the next phase of the nation's destiny is to be decided. I might point out that as New Testament believers we are also presented with spiritual equivalents to Kadesh Barnea. We too are presented with places of major testing. The choices we make during these Kadesh Barnea's determine whether God can move us into his call on our life or whether there will be delay.

Words are an evidence of your faith

God had told the people repeatedly that the land *is* theirs and this was the destiny for which He brought them out of slavery. All they needed to do to obtain their inheritance was to obey Him; be strong and courageous, believing that God will fulfill his word on their behalf.

At God's instruction, Moses selects one man from each tribe to spy out the land and gather intelligence for a military operation. These men return and report that the land is all God promised BUT there are giants that will need to be conquered for them to take possession. Two of the spies, Joshua and Caleb argue that God has promised them victory and He will do as He promised giving them the land. The other ten spies argue against what God said, saying that they can't take the land because the giants are too big and strong, stirring the people to fear and rebel against Moses (and God).

"That night all the people of the community raised their voices and wept aloud. All the Israelites grumbled against Moses and Aaron, and the whole assembly said to them, "If only we had died in Egypt! Or in this desert! Why is the LORD bringing us to this land only to let us fall by the sword? Our wives and children will be taken as plunder. Wouldn't it be better for us to go back to Egypt?" And they said to each other, "We should choose a leader and go back to Egypt." (Numbers 14:1-4)

In essence, the people were saying "Trusting God doesn't make any sense to us! It seems too risky and illogical. Fighting those giants is crazy! We're not doing that! We can't win! What we should really do is control our own destiny and come up with a plan that makes more sense!"

And God responded to their grumbling.

"The LORD said to Moses and Aaron: 'How long will this wicked community grumble against me? I have heard the complaints of these grumbling Israelites.'" (Numbers 14:27)

I once had a Pastor who would regularly say, "The Bible says that God inhabits the praises of his people. If you are God's child and He inhabits your praises, who is inhabiting your grumbling?" He made his point often and I still think about this when tempted to grumble and be ungrateful for what God has given me.

God then instructs Moses to deliver this message to the people.

"As surely as I live, declares the LORD, I will do to you the very things I heard you say: In this desert your bodies will fall—every one of you twenty years old or more who was counted in the census and who has grumbled against me. Not one of you will enter the land I swore with uplifted hand to make your home, except Caleb son of Jephunneh and Joshua son of Nun. As for your children that you said would be taken as plunder, I will bring them in to enjoy the land you have rejected. But you—your bodies will fall in this desert. Your children will be shepherds here for forty years, suffering for your unfaithfulness, until the last of your bodies lies in the desert. For forty years—one year for each of the forty days you explored the land—you will suffer for

your sins and know what it is like to have me against you.' I, the LORD, have spoken, and I will surely do these things to this whole wicked community, which has banded together against me. They will meet their end in this desert; here they will die." (Numbers 14:26-35)

They refused to believe God at his word. Essentially God said "the key to having what I promised to give you wasn't your military prowess, it wasn't the number of fighting men, and it wasn't your weapons or your stature. The key to having all I promised you was to believe me at my word and *act* according to that belief. Now, because you have refused to obey me and choose not to believe what I promised you, I will give you exactly what you do believe. You *said* you would be better off dying in this desert! Well alright then, so be it according to your faith!"

"So the men Moses had sent to explore the land, those who returned and made the whole community grumble against God by spreading a bad report about it, these men responsible for spreading the bad report about the land were struck down and died of a plague before the LORD. Of the men who went to explore the land, only Joshua son of Nun and Caleb son of Jephunneh survived. When Moses reported this to all the Israelites, they mourned bitterly. Early the next morning they went up toward the high hill country. "We have sinned," they said. "We will go up to the place the LORD promised. "But Moses said, "Why are you disobeying the LORD's command? This will not succeed! Do not go up, because the LORD is not with you. You will be defeated by your enemies, for the Amalekites and Canaanites will face you there. Because you have turned away from the LORD, He will not be with you and you will fall by the sword." Nevertheless, in their presumption they went up toward the high hill country, though neither Moses nor the ark of the LORD's covenant moved from the camp. Then the Amalekites and Canaanites who lived in that hill country came down and attacked them and beat them down all the way to Hormah." (Numbers 14:36-44)

> *"Talk what we will of faith, if we do not trust and rely upon Him, we do not believe in Him."*
>
> ~ Anthony Farindon ~

Their destiny became the desert

As a result of their unbelief, the Israelites were forced to wander around in the desert like nomads until all those who refused to believe God and fight in faith for what He promised them were dead. This meant every male except for Joshua and Caleb.

Just as with the Israelites, we Christians have been delivered from "Egypt." Most of us, however, are wandering the desert. God is supplying our every need, but we have never entered our Promised Land, the Spirit-filled life where we have victory over our besetting sin. The sin that God asks us to fight looks foreboding and too difficult to conquer. The fight will require deep sacrifice our part, denying our flesh and trusting God. We reason, "we have all the material comforts and distractions of our community here to ease our difficulty, so even though the Promised Land sounds great; we aren't convinced it's worth the effort. Spiritually, the desert may be a dry and thirsty existence but at least we don't have to risk anything and engage in a fight!"

Many men refuse to seriously address sexual sin because we don't really believe God means what he says in the Bible. The promises He gives us are so mind-boggling. Just the idea of becoming "holy" and having dominion over our sinful natures seems so impossible that we don't even really try. We allow culture to set the standard and we judge our sinfulness by comparing it with others rather than the word of God. The sheer number of porn addicts and divorce within the Church are evidence that this is true.

As a result of our lack of belief, we are destined to wander the spiritual desert, living a dry and dusty Christian experience, hoping and wanting to believe that God's grace will cover a life resigned to enmeshment with sin. We choose to rest in a confession proclaimed years before as evidence that we are right with God. Our hope becomes that words once spoken will provide us a ticket into heaven when our earthly bodies finally fail us and we drop to the sand in exhaustion and die. However, for those that are truly children of God, we cannot embrace our sin. It is not our earthly destiny.

Chapter 7 | Shadows of Freedom

"Get Real" Questions for discussion with other men:

Can you relate to the "Joy" of the Israelites in leaving "Egypt"? Would you be willing to share your salvation experience with the group?

Since you've been saved, have you experienced God attempting to test and grow your faith and trust in him? How? How have you responded?

Since you've been saved, have you had times where you sought comfort in old, sinful behaviors? Why do you think you have done this?

In relating to this story of God's testing of his people's hearts, what has kept you from entering the Promised Land and defeating your (sin) giants? What are you unwilling to trust Him with?

Chapter 8 | The Desert is Meant to Kill you

"Any concept of grace that makes us feel more comfortable sinning is not biblical grace. God's grace never encourages us to live in sin; on the contrary, it empowers us to say no to sin and yes to truth." [1]

"Brothers and sisters, I could not address you as people who live by the Spirit but as people who are still worldly — mere infants in Christ. I gave you milk, not solid food, for you were not yet ready for it. Indeed, you are still not ready. You are still worldly." (1 Corinthians 3:1-3)

The first stage of the Christian life is that of being born again, our freedom from Egypt and the passing through the Red Sea; our acceptance of Christ as our savior and our water baptism into the body of Christ, his Church. This is a time of celebration and joyful gratitude, realizing that we have forgiveness of sin and right standing with God as we enter a new life filled with hope and promise.

In transitioning from the old life to the new we begin growing in knowledge and strength, we learn to walk as a toddler in the body of Christ. This is the desert where God meets our needs and feeds us "manna" that sustains us. He provides for us pastors and teachers, and a Church family to give us "solid food" for our growth in knowledge and awareness of God.

Initially, we often look to others to help us determine what is appropriate Christian behavior. Our leaders help us set the boundaries necessary to avoid stumbling in our newfound liberties or falling back under the influence of corrupting personalities. We readily look to the local members of the body of Christ to help us as we make mistakes and need help cleaning up the messes we make or have made in the past that must now be dealt with.

If we survive in our faith, it is usually somewhere in this stage of our Christian growth (which can take decades) that we begin to realize the need for a deeper work to be done in our lives if we are to obtain victory over our besetting sins. We come to the realization that it is easier to walk with Christ in name than in action. For desires to be transformed, something more of Christ is needed beyond our own efforts and willpower if we are to walk out the life we have been called to.

This is the work of the desert, to show us that we can't transform our desires and overcome sin by our own effort. Unfortunately, many refuse to believe that they are called to overcome sin. Instead they choose to comfort themselves with the thought that there is no need because our choosing to sin is covered by the grace of God. Then, secure in this thought, they settle into the nomadic life that comes from desert living, distracting and comforting themselves with activities, pleasures and the pursuit of worldly possessions.

The very real danger that exists from remaining in this place, and it is inevitable, is that you become lukewarm, neither hot nor cold. Church becomes a social exercise, a place to be entertained or something you do for the kids, but you have no burning desire to truly worship God with obedience. Your devotions and prayer time, if you have them at all, become more of a ritual or duty where the relationship of God is no longer sensed. There may be a sense of guilt about this lack of love, but not enough to really seek God for change. You may even come to fear, if you are honest, that doing so might mean you have to give up a sin you really love, and so you settle your hope on the grace of God and relax. You become passive in the pursuit of your relationship with God.

When your desire for God is waning and you recognize that your relationship with God isn't what it should be, this is an awareness brought to you by the Holy Spirit. If you don't listen to his voice and press into God but instead choose to become complacent, you open yourself up to the temptation and desire for the pleasures of Egypt.

The Christian who "settles down" in the desert becomes a carnal Christian, susceptible and often falling into the temptations of the world. Unfortunately, this condition is prevalent in the American Church. The Church both collectively and individually is not walking in the Spirit and most of us are not living perceptively different than our worldly counterparts. We are wandering the desert. If we don't embrace the lessons the desert is meant to teach us we are doomed to die here, never seeing the fullness of God's blessings for us.

The enemy sees you coming

For the Israelites, forty long years in the desert have passed. All the people who grumbled against God and refused to believe his promise to lead the nation in defeating the enemies of the land are now dead.

Moses begins to move the people toward the Promised Land for the second time. As they approach the edge of the Promised Land, the Israelites are attacked by the Canaanite King Arad, (Numbers 21) who takes some of the people captive. It is interesting to note that when this happens, the Bible says,

The "Israelites called on God *making a vow* to completely destroy this enemy if God would give them victory and He listened to them, and delivered the enemy into their hands and they completely destroyed the inhabitants and their towns." (v. 2, 3)

The Israelites did not initiate this battle, the enemy did. As the Gospel takes root in us, and we mature and grow stronger in our Christian walk and in relationship with Christ, we will naturally progress in walking in the Spirit. As we approach those places in the strength of God where we have failed God in the past, the enemy will proactively attack us in an effort to intimidate and discourage us.

Chapter 21 says that King Arad did take some of them captive. We will meet with defeats, but this is where, instead of giving up or running to the pastor, we get on our face in believing faith before God and call on Him to give us the victory he has promised, and then we step forward and engage the enemy!

As you would expect, the enemy doesn't give up after one small defeat, and as Israel continues to move toward the Promised Land they are attacked again by Og and Sihon, kings of the Amorite nations. God gives the Israelites crushing victories over these kings as well.

After these initial victories, the Israelites are gaining confidence and have now marched around Edom and through the Amorite Kingdoms and are headed through the edge of Moab toward Jericho. Balak, the King of Moab and Midian is becoming fearful of Israel. He has been hearing how all the nations are falling before Israel and her God with relative ease. In near panic he hires Balaam, a prophet/sorcerer to come to his aid. He offers Balaam money and asks him to place a curse on the Israelites in an effort to find a way to stop their advance.

The Israelites are now nearly to the border, and about to enter the Promised Land for which they have wandered the desert so long. King Balak is desperate to stop them, seeing that he is no match for the God of Israel. King Balaak knows Israel is going to be unstoppable unless he can find a way, any way, to remove God's blessing from them.

The Bible states that God wouldn't allow Balaam to place a curse on his chosen people, however the sorcerer still wants to get his money from the king. In an effort to placate King Balaak he shares some inside information on *a sure-fire strategy* to get the nation of Israel to *bring a curse on itself.*

The seduction of a curse

Balaam's strategy is so simple in its implementation, yet so powerful that our enemy still uses this strategy to negate the power of Christian men to this day. Balaam instructs Balaak to use the beautiful women of Moab to seduce the men of Israel into immoral sexuality and idol worship. Then, God would become so outraged over their spiritual adultery against Him that He would remove His blessing from them.

Just as then, this strategy is highly effective, as is evident by the revelation that 60% of the men currently in Church are addicted to pornography. Seduction is everywhere we turn; it is targeted at our young boys and men, neutering their spiritual sensitivity and power through the curse of addiction. When we embrace sexual sin in any of its many forms, *we bring a curse on ourselves.* We open the door for our enemy to access our spiritual lives, our marriages and our families.

The plan very nearly succeeded. The men were seduced and lured into immoral sexuality and idol worship. Numbers 25:3 says that,

"Israel yoked themselves with the Baal of Peor and the anger of the Lord burned against them."

Baal means "lord" or "possessor" and peor means "opening" or "wide opening." Part of the Baal Peor worship was defecating before the idol as an offering and committing drunken sexual acts.

As a result of this seduction, the people cursed themselves and the Lord's anger brought a plague upon the people of Israel. Moses was instructed to put to death every person who had instigated or participated in "yoking themselves to Baal Peor." Once he did, the plague was stopped, but not before 24,000 people died! God takes sexual sin and idolatry very, very seriously.

The last battle of the desert

It is interesting to note that Moses' final battle directive as the leader of Israel was to exact the vengeance of God upon the Moabites. Under God's command, Moses released the fighting men of Israel upon the nations and kings of Moab and Midian for seducing his people into sexual sin and idol worship. They killed every man including Balaam the prophet/sorcerer, and returned victorious with the animals, possessions, women and children as the spoils of the battle. Including the women who had seduced them! Moses becomes angered that the fighting men are *so spiritually dull* as to take into captivity the very women that seduced the nation into sexual sin in the first place and commands that every woman who is not a virgin be killed.

"Primarily, God is not bound to punish sin; he is bound to destroy sin. The only vengeance worth having on sin is to make the sinner himself its executioner."

~ *George McDonald* ~

One of the devil's most effective strategies against the Christian man is sexual sin. It is amazing how, just like these warriors, we are so blind and passive to the cultural seduction we allow ourselves to be exposed to. For us to be holy men we must be ruthless in dealing with this sin and its various forms of entry into our lives. It is a hook from which it is hard to escape and it has eternal consequences. We cannot harbor even an infinitesimal part of it!

Why is this particular sin battle so intense? When going to battle, a wise general will seek to attack at strategic, key points that will expose and weaken his foe rather than coming at the enemy's strongest points. Once the key defenses have been breached, the territory will then be occupied and further advance prepared. Once weakened, the occupied country must send reinforcements to strengthen and retake the area or concede the territory to the enemy and focus their efforts elsewhere. Oftentimes they must divert resources from their strongpoints to counter that attack, thus further depleting their resources. The advancing army will commit troops to holding these areas because the ultimate victory depends on it!

Our enemy has committed a huge portion of his energy and resources to the area of sexual compromise in the lives of God's men. The temptations are everywhere and the vilest of his work is readily available to any child with a smartphone. This is a stronghold in territory he is dedicated to holding because the ramifications of the victory are so huge; not just the physical consequences, but this is how he causes us to suffer defeat in the spiritual realm as well.

This strategy of sexual seduction was one of the enemy's greatest weapons in keeping the Israelites from having the presence of God lead them. Having God's presence and leading was the ONLY way they could succeed! I believe with all my heart that the battle to overcome sexual sin is a war that every Christian man must fight. It is a key battle in experiencing the tangible presence of God reigning in our hearts, enabling us to live holy lives and operate effectively in his kingdom.

"Do you not know that the wicked will not inherit the kingdom of God? *Do not be deceived:* Neither the sexually immoral nor idolaters nor adulterers nor male prostitutes nor homosexual offenders" (1 Corinthians 6:9)

We cannot enter the Spirit-filled life until we are willing to surrender all of our desires to Christ. God cannot trust you with his Spirit and his presence if you refuse to grow up. A baby, immature Christian has a weak character and wants what it wants NOW and is not willing to apply effort or deny the gratification of its flesh. A Christian man of God is one who is developing the character that is fully submitted to pursuing life according to God's direction. A Christian man defers or denies the desires of his flesh to the purpose of following Jesus.

"Whoever wants to be my disciple must deny themselves...and follow me." (Luke 9:23)

It's time to grow up and become a weapon in the hand of God. We cannot take the land without God and he will not take it for us; He expects our participation. We must be a weapon in the hand of God if there is to be victory. Too often we try to enter the battle based on our tactics with God as a weapon in our hand!

We say, "God, here are my battle plans for the day; pay raise, promotion, new house etc., I ask that you walk with me and bless me." But God responds, "Here are my battle plans for the day, obey my commands, walk in love and holiness. I desire for you to walk with me and I will bless you!" There is a subtle, but worlds apart, difference.

The Bible teaches that there are only two choices for the Christian...walk in the Spirit or in the flesh. A soldier under the authority of his commander is either under an active command or he is absent without permission to be on leave. Many men simply want to show up on Sunday and get the affirmation that comes from looking the part of the bride of Christ. Just like the men of Israel who believed they could pursue the women of Moab without consequence, this man wants the comfort of believing he has eternal life without any discomfort, repentance or accountability to God. Believing this is even possible is a delusion from our enemy and these men are already his prisoners of war.

> "Those who belong to Christ Jesus have crucified the flesh with its passions and desires." (Galatians 5:24)

Crucifixion is not instant death. In fact, it was typically painfully slow and tortuous. Once the victim had been nailed or tied to the cross he had been crucified, but he is not dead. Death could take anywhere from hours to days as the person slowly suffocated. The Romans designed this type of death to be excruciatingly slow and agonizing in order to serve as an example to anyone who would rebel against their authority.

When it comes to our flesh, if we are in Christ we have been crucified, but our sin nature is still alive and gasping for breath, desperately trying to stay alive and exert its influence over us; but it is slowly losing strength. With every gasping breath it takes, our delight should be to watch it die and ensure, by daily dependence on Christ, that we give no life to it.

Chapter 8 | The desert is meant to kill you

"Get Real" Questions for discussion with other men:

Have you relied on grace to avoid dealing with sin in your life?

How would you rate your relationship with God on a scale from 1 - 10? How has not dealing with your sin affected your relationship with God?

How do you feel about today's seductions in relation to the "women of Moab strategy" used against the Israelites?

Are you, or have you been "absent without leave" as a Christian man, looking the part but avoiding the battle?

How do you "choose" to walk in the Spirit? How do you "choose" to walk in the flesh?

Chapter 9 | Killing Fleas

"A person who wholly follows the Lord is one who believes that the promises of God are trustworthy, that He is with His people, and that they are well able to overcome." [1]

"For our struggle is not against flesh and blood, but against the rulers, against the authorities, against the powers of this dark world and against the spiritual forces of evil in the heavenly realms." (Ephesians 6:12)

Many of us were led to Christ through the preaching of a pastor or an evangelist, and most of the time we have great respect and love for that man. This is understandable for the bible refers to them as a spiritual father (1 Corinthians 4:15). We tend to revere him and follow his teaching closely as he disciples us as a father in the Lord. However, the evangelist or pastor's job is not to have faith on your behalf or hear God's voice for you. He is there to encourage and mentor your direct relationship with Jesus so that you may learn to hear and discern God's voice and leading for yourself.

Your ultimate desire should be to know Christ intimately and learn to trust the Holy Spirit to lead and direct your life. As great as Moses was in his role of leading the people out of bondage, he was not the man

God had chosen to lead his people into the land where giants are fought.

God's choice for a new leader

When Moses died, Joshua was God's choice to lead his people into the Promised Land. The wonderful book named after him chronicles the Israelites' entry into the land led by Joshua, a type of Christ. The very name Joshua (meaning deliverer) is the same as Yehoshua, Jesus. Jesus, by the Holy Spirit, is the *only one* who can lead us to the place where no other man can take us in our walk with God. Without Jesus leading us into battle there is no victory and no walking in the dominion over sin that we are meant to have.

As we prepare to look at the crossing over into the Promised Land I want to remind you that the journey from Egypt to Canaan could have been accomplished in a matter of days. However, it took decades because of a key principle still in effect today. *They were held back by God Himself from taking the land because of their sin, namely the sin of unbelief and pride.* They refused to believe that God would (and could) lead them to conquer the enemies of the land. Instead, they chose to believe that their own way of thinking was more believable and real than trusting and obeying God.

Rather than looking to and trusting the God who just days before had opened the Red Sea to make a way of escape and drowned their enemies, they were looking at the size of the enemy before them. The Bible describes them as giants. The Israelites were painfully aware of, and focused on their own weakness, lack of weaponry, military skill and experience. Their fighting experience consisted of ...well...nothing. They had been slaves for the last 400 years; they had never fought an enemy!

When we are first brought to salvation we also have no idea how to fight spiritual battles, and our belief is that we have to fight our spiritual battles over sin in the power of our own will and determination, relying on our skill and expertise. This is not true. We must learn to fight in God's kingdom, in God's way, and there is much to learn from the experience of the Israelites under the leadership of Joshua.

"The only way to learn great faith is to endure great trials."

~ George Muller ~

When we are immature Christians, God provides our every need just as he provided water and manna daily to the Israelites for 40 years. During this time in the desert He was not just meeting their needs, He was teaching them truths they needed to know. He grew in them a desire to serve and be obedient. But the Israelites were about to learn that God doesn't just add his power to human effort, He does it all, yet, He allows and *requires* us to participate in the victory. Our victory comes through obedience to God and a faith that clings to God's word as more real than what our senses communicate to us. A faith that is willing to step out in action.

Preparations

The book of Joshua opens with God speaking to Joshua saying,

"Be strong and very courageous. Be careful to obey all the law my servant Moses gave you; do not turn from it to the right or to the left, that you may be successful wherever you go. Keep this Book of the Law always on your lips; meditate on it day and night, so that you may be careful to do everything written in it. Then you will be prosperous and successful. Have I not commanded you? Be strong and courageous. Do not be afraid; do not be discouraged, for the LORD your God will be with you wherever you go." (Joshua 1:7-9)

God says, "All right now, it's go time....stir yourself up! This is what you have been waiting for all these years. I have told you what you need to do to have my presence with you and defeat your enemies. Make sure you do exactly as I have directed. I have given you my word, and whose word is more trustworthy than mine? If you do as I have instructed, my presence will rest on you in everything you pursue."

"So Joshua ordered the officers of the people: 'Go through the camp and tell the people, 'Get your provisions ready. Three days from now you will cross the Jordan here to go in and take possession of the land the LORD your God is giving you for your own." (Joshua 1:10-11)

Joshua then sends two spies to check out the city of Jericho, the first enemy stronghold. It happens to be a strongly fortified city just on the other side of the river. The men return and tell Joshua,

"The Lord has surely given the whole land into our hands; all the people are melting in fear because of us." (Joshua 2:24)

As the people are camped at the edge of the Jordan River and preparing to cross, Joshua commands the people,

"Consecrate yourselves, for tomorrow the Lord will do amazing things among you." (Joshua 3:5)

Then Joshua said to the Israelites,

"Come here and listen to the words of the LORD your God. This is how you will know that the living God is among you...See, the ark of the covenant of the Lord of all the earth will go into the Jordan ahead of you...And as soon as the priests who carry the ark of the LORD, the Lord of all the earth, set foot in the Jordan, its waters flowing downstream will be cut off and stand up in a heap." (Joshua 3:11-13)

The next day, it happened just as Joshua said and the people passed through the Jordan River on dry ground.

Are you willing to get low?

Remember what the Apostle Paul said about the Old Testament.

"Now all these things happened unto them by way of example, (as a type or pattern) and are written for our admonition (authoritative counsel or warning), upon whom the ends of the world are come." (1 Corinthians 10:11)

And in reference to the crossing of the Red Sea, 1 Corinthians 10: 1-2 says,

"For I do not want you to be ignorant of the fact, brothers and sisters that our ancestors... all passed through the sea. They were all baptized into Moses in the cloud and in the sea.

The baptism of Moses represents a change in our *status or standing* that frees us from the slavery to sin. But it does not represent a change of our hearts' desires. What is needed for a real relationship is a true love of Jesus and a deep desire to fellowship with Him and live this life according to his ways, not ours. This requires a work of the Holy Spirit. As we will see, this is what is symbolized by the crossing of the Jordan River and is a necessity for overcoming sin and entry into a new way of living in a relationship with God. It represents the presence of God living *in* us, without which there can be no true and lasting heart change.

This is so crucial to understand. On the cross Christ died so that our sins could be forgiven that we might be clean before God and fit for the Holy Spirit to dwell in us in union as one spirit, fused together. So many Christians stop with accepting Jesus as the payment for sin. Not only did He die for you, He also rose again for you, returning to heaven so his Holy Spirit could live *in those* who yield to him in obedience and *ask* to be filled and controlled by His Spirit. (Luke 11:13)

The Hebrew word for the Jordan River means "descending" or "descend-er." It is interesting that the location where the Israelite's crossed the Jordan River is the same place where Jesus was baptized by John the Baptist. This place of baptism is where the Holy Spirit visibly descended upon Jesus just prior to the start of his ministry. Just as the nation of Israel's experience of God's power on them changed after their decent into the Jordon River, Jesus' ministry was marked with power after He was baptized in the Jordan. Jesus was about to enter the battle for all mankind and his submission to the Holy Spirit was necessary.

For the Spirit of God to live in us in power we must purposely descend in humility and submission to God, saying just as Jesus did, "not my will but yours be done." There is no way through the Jordan into the life of the Spirit except for our pride to be brought low in submission to Jesus, our King.

Jesus went out of his way to be baptized by John. The journey from Galilee to meet John the Baptist was about 60 miles. John's baptism was a baptism of repentance, and true repentance requires deep, sorrowful contrition and penitence for sin.

Jesus, however, was sinless and had no need of repentance, so why did He go so far out of his way to purposely model this example, particularly in this location? Why did this event mark the start of his ministry? I believe it was to show not only the absolute need for repentance and sorrow over our sin, but also to let us know it is a necessary requirement for the Spirit of

God to be present in our lives if we are to walk in dominion over sin. Often when we are first saved, we are excited to change our ways and live for Christ and so we exert our best effort. There comes a place where the Holy Spirit allows us to see that this is impossible without a fresh and deeper surrender to his power working in us to enable our obedience through faith.

Before we seek the power and presence of the Holy Spirit we need to consecrate ourselves just as Joshua, a type of Jesus, asked the Israelites to do. Consecration means a dedication to a specific person or purpose. Before we get married, becoming one in flesh with a wife, we men wrestle with thoughts such as "is this the right one? Is this a sacrifice I am willing to make? Can I be faithful to her my whole life? Am I willing to lay aside my wants, lusts and desires for the needs of my wife and future family?" This questioning is necessary in surrendering to God as well. Can I really commit?

Cat tossing

I used to have a fluffy little gray and white cat named Jack. He was a pampered house kitty who didn't have front claws. I had them removed so he wouldn't tear up my furniture. As a result, I never let him outside. He was quite snugly and loving, bordering on obsessively needy which, as one of his mildly annoying traits, pales in comparison to his very, very loud meow.

One night, about 3 am as I was snuggled in bed, Jack began to cry...LOUDLY. He obviously saw something through the window and was trying to either get its attention or tell it to "get off my turf." I tried to distract him by taking him back to bed with me but I couldn't get him to shut up and stay away from the window. I was losing sleep and finally at the end of my patience I angrily muttered, "You want to talk to whatever is out there!? Then have at it!" as I flipped him out the door and into the woods behind my place.

Well, when Jack didn't come back the next day I felt bad about losing my temper and had to repent. I began praying that he was ok and would come home safe. When I finally found him three days later, he was filthy. His long fur was matted and clumpy. As soon as he saw me he started his meow-howl. He had diarrhea and looked scrawny and beat up. I took him home and gave him some treat-food which he wolfed down so fast he promptly threw up. I was feeling pretty bad about myself and my short temper.

I cleaned him up and thought he was going to be fine but it wasn't long before I noticed him "scratching," and within a few days I discovered he had brought home a flea or two. Not knowing much about fleas, (remember, pampered indoor cat) I didn't take it too seriously, after all it's just a little flea, right? I'll get some "stuff" and kill 'em...no problem!

Initially I bought some over the counter flea killer you squirt on the animal's neck once a month. I was trying to save some money and that flea stuff can get expensive so I went for the cheaper brand. It wasn't long before I was giving it to him weekly in an effort to get rid of the fleas and it still wasn't working. He was slinking around, not eating much and his fur was greasy from all the flea goop I had been covering him with. It looked like upping the dosage from monthly to weekly was making him sick. If that wasn't bad enough it didn't seem to be killing the fleas.

Four months passed and nothing was working. My cat still had fleas and I started to find flea bites on my legs and would catch the occasional flea hopping around the house. I needed to get drastic! I decided I would drown the fleas by shampooing the cat. I bought some flea shampoo, put two inches of warm water in the kitchen sink and grabbed Jack by the scruff of his neck. I DID actually get him in the sink but I was never able to get him really wet above his lower back.

As I gave it my best effort, I imagined all the fleas running for higher ground around his neck where, try as I might, I couldn't wash effectively. He was contorting and howling in an effort to get out of the water (my neighbors probably thought I was killing some wild animal). I got wetter than the cat and with my kitchen a wreck, I gave up on the shampoo idea.

My next idea was to cut off all his hair. I tried clippers like the ones you trim your beard with but his fur was way too thick, so I got out the scissors and started clipping away. Needless to say that didn't work either and my cat ended up looking like a circus freak.

By this time, I was getting really desperate to kill the fleas! In the end, eight months later, I'd spent hundreds of dollars on various flea remedies, bombed my house several times, and was vacuuming the entire house every day in an attempt to get rid of those "bleeping"

FLEAS! I am telling you I had grown to the point where I HATED fleas!

Sexual sin is worse than fleas

Here is the spiritual lesson I learned. I had recovered my little kitty from an environment where fleas have free and uncontrolled reign. I brought him back into my home where fleas *should not* rule and *should not* be seen. However, just because my kitty was free from the dominion of the flea kingdom didn't mean the fleas would quietly go away. I had to fight to destroy each and every flea if the advancement of the flea army in my home was to be stopped. I learned the hard way that there are inevitable consequences to passive or halfhearted animosity towards the tiny flea.

If you want to get rid of fleas you need to count the cost upfront, pay the price and go all in with everything you've got and nuke the little parasitic bloodsuckers. If you don't, you are wasting your time! When it comes to even one little flea, there can be no mercy, even if you have to nearly kill the cat!!! If you leave just one baby flea alive it won't be long before you have a brand new flea herd snacking on the cat and hopping around the house.

When it comes to conquering personal sin, especially sexual sin, you will not, you cannot have victory without the full power of Holy Spirit and fighting the battle God's way. You cannot approach sexual sin casually sipping a Slurpee in one hand and expect to win. You don't get to say "God, I only want enough to kill off my lust for pornography. I'm not too worried about my thought life, so just a little dab will do me!"

There can be no compromise with the enemy. And conversely, there is no partial surrender of your life to the Lordship of Christ in this area. You cannot serve two masters, and if you aren't fully surrendered to Christ or choose to avoid this battle, then like the lyrics from the Rush song Freewill, "If you choose not to decide, you still have made a choice." The word of God lays out two choices, walk in the flesh or walk in the Spirit. If you aren't in the Spirit, you're in the flesh.

Before we ask God to do a work in us, we need to go through the process of realizing that if we are asking God to give us the power of his Holy Spirit to conquer our sexual sin, he will expect us to be obedient with what He is giving us; actively and aggressively pursuing every area in becoming a weapon of vengeance in the eradication our personal sin. Are you ready to be ruthless and do whatever it takes? If not, you are wasting your time.

Many men aren't ready to surrender this area completely. We each need to go through a soul-searching period, a time of prayer and honestly ask ourselves, "Am I really willing to give up control of my life to the Spirit of God? Am I really ready and willing to give up my favorite sin(s)? Am I willing to go all the way? How radical am I willing to get in dealing with my sin? Am I willing to 'cut off my hand or pluck out my eye?' Am I willing to do *whatever* God asks of me?"

Chapter 9 | Killing Fleas

"Get Real" Questions for discussion with other men:

Re-read Joshua 1:7-9, do you think this promise applies to you today?

The Jordan River means "descending." As the river opened to let them through to the other side, the Israelites had to descend into the riverbed to cross over into the land. As an analogy what might be the implications for us as modern Christians?

Why do you think Jesus went so far out of his way to be baptized by John the Baptist?

Do you have any spiritual fleas that you have been unable to kill on your own?

How would you answer the question, "What am I afraid to do or give up in obedience to Christ in conquering my sin?"

Chapter 10 | Obedience Matters

"...he who believes is obedient and only who is obedient believes" [1]

"In Him you were also circumcised with a circumcision not performed by human hands. Your whole self-ruled by the flesh was put off when you were circumcised by Christ...through your faith in the working of God." (Ephesians 6:12)

The Israelites have now crossed over into enemy territory, their first steps into the land of promise. The Bible says that when the kings on that side of the river heard about the Jordan River parting for the Israelites, allowing them to enter their land, their hearts melted and they had no courage to face God's people.

The book of Joshua tells us two very interesting things happened at this time. God stopped providing manna for his people, and God told Joshua to circumcise the men. The manna in the wilderness was God's provision for his people as they wandered through the desert. This represents the need of modern baby Christians' for constant care and feeding.

With the crossing of the Jordan River, God would now begin providing in a different way for his people. They had reached the place where, rather than eat the same food as everyone else, they could gather, grow and eat the food that they chose. In essence, they were now empowered to harvest from all that God provided. They were now responsible to find and choose food for their own nourishment.

For the New Testament believer, God supplies pastors, teachers and a Church community to support and feed us as baby Christians. They are provided to help us discern our place in the Church community and assist us as we learn to walk in the Spirit. They will always be a part of our life but the Bible says the Holy Spirit once received and indwelling, will teach us all things (John 14:26). As we mature, we become individually responsible for the disciplines that feed and nourish an intimate fellowship and relationship with God.

Just as water baptism is meant to be an outward sign or evidence of our spiritual identification with Christ's death, the physical circumcision commanded by God was to be their outward representation of his spiritual covenant with his people. Male circumcision was to be a sign of Israel's covenant with God, showing that they were his people and fully committed to this covenant.

For us, this covenant is reflected in a circumcision of our heart. This "cutting" of the heart is identifying with Christ through our becoming one with the Holy Spirit. Just as there is no birth without the involvement of the male organ, here circumcised in covenant to God, there is no true spiritual creation or "born again" life without a heart circumcised by the Holy Spirit toward God. For a born again believer, the circumcised heart is manifested outwardly by repentance, obedience and inwardly by a heart sensitive towards God.

Proverbs 4:23 says, "Above all else, guard your heart, for it is the wellspring of life."

The spiritual life, being truly born again, comes from the indwelling Holy Spirit and is a creative work of God, the new birth. When the Holy Spirit fills you and joins to your spirit, your desires change. The change sometimes follows slowly, but the heart's desire *must* change if you have the Holy Spirit in you. If the desires of your heart aren't progressively becoming more like those of Jesus and increasingly resistant to sin, you have reason to be concerned about the reality of your salvation.

Taking Jericho

After circumcising all the men, they camped in the plains of Jericho and celebrated Passover. They had a party. The Bible says the city of Jericho closed up their gates and no one came in or left for fear of the Israelites.

Then the LORD said to Joshua,

"See, I have delivered Jericho into your hands, along with its king and its fighting men. March around the city once with all the armed men. Do this for six days. Have seven priests carry trumpets of rams' horns in front of the ark. On the seventh day, march around the city seven times, with the priests blowing the trumpets. When you hear them sound a long blast on the trumpets, have the whole army give a loud shout; then the wall of the city will collapse and the army will go up, everyone straight in." (Joshua 6:2-5)

Now if fighting giants seemed absurd, this would be a true test of the Israelites commitment to obedience! Can you imagine walking around an enemy city every day in silence while the people on the wall looked down at you? I would be thinking, "Ok? What in the world are we doing walking around this city every day? This sure doesn't seem very productive! I can't believe this is what God is asking us to do!"

It is interesting to note that in verse 10, Joshua specifically instructs the men to march *in silence, not to speak one word!* I can't help but think that Joshua may have been recalling what happened 40 years earlier when the people grumbled against God!

In obedience, they did what God asked and the book says,

"On the seventh day, they got up at daybreak and marched around the city seven times in the same manner, except that on that day they circled the city seven times. The seventh time around, when the priests sounded the trumpet blast, Joshua commanded the army, "Shout! For the LORD has given you the city! The city and all that is in it are to be devoted to the LORD. Only Rahab the prostitute and all who are with her in her house shall be spared, because she hid the spies we sent. *But keep away from the devoted things, so that you will not bring about your own destruction by taking any of them. Otherwise you will make the camp of Israel liable to destruction and bring trouble on it. All the silver and gold and the articles of bronze and iron*

are sacred to the LORD and must go into his treasury."
(Joshua 6:16 -19)

After the shout, the walls fell down and the Israelites destroyed the city just as God promised.

God must be first

Here is another principle and evidence of a surrendered life and outward evidence of an obedient heart that trusts God. The entirety of our lives must be devoted to God; our worship, our time and our money.

After the battle, as they were gathering all the gold, silver and bronze for the treasury of the Lord, a man named Achan, (which means troublemaker) kept a robe and some gold and silver for himself and hid it in his tent. God had warned the warriors through Joshua that keeping what was to be devoted to Him would bring about not only the offender's destruction but also open up the possibility of trouble for the nation of the Israel as a whole.

The nation, unaware of Achan's sin, moved deeper into the land. Joshua, hearing the report from his advance scouts that the city of Ai would fall easily, sent only 3,000 men to attack the city.

Interestingly, Joshua didn't consult with God before executing his battle plan against Ai. With their recent victory, he must have been feeling pretty confident, thinking "we got this one, no sweat!" He must have felt with Ai being such a small city, they could handle it. No problem, no need to consult God first. However, they were soundly routed, and with the defeat Joshua *knew* that God had not gone with them; he was distraught.

That night, Joshua got alone with God and fell on his face. He tore his clothes in distress and asked God "Why you have done this to us!? Why have you not gone with us!?" God's response is telling for those of us who claim his name.

"The LORD said to Joshua, "Stand up! What are you doing down on your face? Israel has sinned; they have violated my covenant, which I commanded them to keep. They have taken some of the devoted things; they have stolen, they have lied, they have put them with their own possessions. *That is why the Israelites cannot stand against their enemies; they turn their backs and run because they have been made liable to destruction. I will not be with you anymore unless you destroy whatever is among you that is devoted to destruction.* Go, consecrate the people. Tell them, consecrate yourselves in preparation for tomorrow; for this is what the LORD, the God of Israel, says: There are devoted things among you, Israel. **You cannot stand against your enemies until you remove them.**"

God responded, saying in essence, "Quit blaming me for this! You have brought this on yourselves. Get off your face and deal with your sin like a man of God! **Recommit yourselves and deal with your sin**!"

Achan's humiliation

The next day, God led Joshua to have the people pass before him, tribe by tribe, slowly narrowing it down to the tribe of Judah. Then each clan of Judah passed before him and it was narrowed down to the Zerahites. Then each family among the Zerahites passed before him and it was narrowed down to the Zimri family. Then each man in the Zimri family passed before him and it was narrowed to a man named Achan.

Then Joshua said to Achan,

"My son, give glory to the LORD, the God of Israel, and honor Him. Tell me what you have done; do not hide it from me." Achan replied, "It is true! I have sinned against the LORD, the God of Israel. This is what I have done: When I saw in the plunder a beautiful robe from Babylonia, two hundred shekels of silver and a bar of gold weighing fifty shekels, I *coveted* them and took them. They are hidden in the ground inside my tent, with the silver underneath." So Joshua sent messengers, and they ran to the tent, and there it was, hidden in his tent, with the silver underneath. (Joshua 7:19)

It is revealing that God exposed Achan's sin *in front of all the people*, using Joshua to elicit an open air confession from him. Achan confessed to "coveting" the treasure and taking it for himself. The word "covet" means to desire greatly and is synonymous with lust. When it comes to sexual sin, God also requires that we confess our sins to each other. If we do, He promises He will heal us, forgive us and restore power to our spiritual life (James 5:16). The Bible continues,

"Then Joshua, together with all Israel, took Achan son of Zerah, the silver, the robe, the gold bar, his sons and daughters, his cattle, donkeys and sheep, his tent and all that he had, to the Valley of Achor." and there, they stoned them all. (Joshua 7:24 -26)

In God's view there can be *no mercy* when it comes to eradicating sin from his people. Everything associated with Achan was killed and buried under a heap of rocks.

In the New Testament Jesus speaks of Himself as a "stone" saying to those who don't produce the fruit He desires,

"He who falls on this stone will be broken to pieces, but he on whom it falls will be crushed." (Matthew 21:43, 44)

Then the LORD said to Joshua,

"Do not be afraid; do not be discouraged. Take the whole army with you, and go up and attack Ai. For I have delivered into your hands the king of Ai, his people, his city and his land. You shall do to Ai and its king as you did to Jericho and its king, *except that you may carry off their plunder and livestock for yourselves.* (Joshua 8:1-2)

"The true follower of Christ will not ask, "If I embrace this truth, what will it cost me?" Rather, he will say, "This is truth. God help me to walk in it."

~ A.W. Tozer ~

If Achan had only been patient and trusted God! If he had only been obedient and done it God's way, the plunder from the next city would have been his for the taking and not just a bar of gold and a robe, but all that he could carry! What a lesson for us! When we try to get what we want using our own logic and wisdom rather than trusting God and being patient, we bring destruction on ourselves and those around us! If we will just follow his instruction and patiently trust that He knows best, we will always get his best which is better than what we can get using our own logic and effort!

"...the LORD bestows favor and honor; no good thing does He withhold from those whose walk is blameless." (Psalm 84:11)

From this point forward in the book of Joshua, defeat in battle is never mentioned again. We learn that God gave the nation rest and they served the Lord for the remainder of Joshua's life. They never lost another battle. Just before his death Joshua gave the people one last warning about the importance of being diligent in faithful obedience toward God. I believe this is warning is just as relevant for us today.

"So be very careful to love the LORD your God...But if you turn away and ally yourselves with the survivors of these nations...and associate with them, then you may be sure that the LORD your God will no longer drive out these nations before you. Instead, **they will become snares and traps for you, until you perish**....You know with all your heart and soul that not one of all the good promises the LORD your God gave you has failed. Every promise has been fulfilled; not one has failed. But just as all the good things the LORD your God has promised you have come to you, so He will bring on you all the evil things He has threatened...If you violate the covenant of the LORD your God, which He commanded you, and go and serve other gods and bow down to them, the LORD's anger will burn against you, and you will quickly perish..." (Joshua 23:11-16)

When it comes to sexual sin we can make no room for it, or it will become a snare and trap that will be used against us...until we perish.

Chapter 10 | Obedience matters

"Get Real" Questions for discussion with other men:

Have you ever consciously asked the Holy Spirit to inhabit your body as his temple, to become one with you? If not, why not?

What does it mean to have a circumcised heart? How do you know if your heart is circumcised towards God?

Why do you think God dealt so harshly with Achan's hidden sin?

Read Joshua's final warning. Should you apply this to your life today and if so, what is God saying through Joshua to you? What changes do you need to make?

Authors note: Please consider providing a review of The Purity Driven Life on Amazon.com.

Chapter 11 | What do you know?

"People to whom sin is just a matter of words, to them salvation is just words too." [1]

*"Not everyone who says to Me, 'Lord, Lord,' will enter the kingdom of heaven, **but he who does the will of My Father who is in heaven will enter.** Many will say to Me on that day, 'Lord, Lord, did we not prophesy in Your name, and in Your name cast out demons, and in Your name perform many miracles?' And then I will declare to them, **'I never knew you;** depart from me, you who practice lawlessness."* (Matt 7:21-23)

There is a delightful woman I worked with for 7 or 8 years, one day while a group of us were working on a project, she mentioned that she suffered from seizures most of her adult life. When I asked why I had never seen her have a seizure during all the time we had worked together, she went on to share; "The seizures usually happen in the evening while at home, but if it ever were to happen at work, here is what to expect. I will lock up like a computer freezing, and then go limp and get glassy-eyed, but don't panic. The seizure will only last about two to three minutes and like a computer rebooting, I'll wake up groggy, having no memory of what happened; otherwise I will be fine".

About a year later, she had a seizure at work. When several of the staff came running into my office in a panic, I calmly said, "Remember, she told us about this... just let her be still for a few minutes and she will be fine."

We found out later that she didn't suffer from seizures at all, but from a syndrome called "Long QT." She actually died in our offices that day. It just so happened that we had a brand new employee who was unaware of the information we had been given the prior year. She immediately called 911 and started CPR. Because of her prompt action, the paramedics were able to resuscitate my coworker and get her heart beating again. She was in a coma for about a week and missed over a month of work in recovery.

My point you ask? Based on the information I had been given, I felt confident in my judgment to just let her be still for a few minutes, believing she would be fine. There is just one small but vitally important point; the knowledge upon which I based my decision would have ensured her death! Because I trusted the source of the information, I was willing to risk my coworker's life on what I believed was accurate information.

The problem was, my source gave us the wrong advice because she didn't have correct information, and so both us were wrong! Very sincere, but deadly wrong! Sometimes we think we know the truth, and because we trust the person who delivered it, we never make any effort to verify the accuracy or truth for ourselves. I believe that is what happened in Matthew 7 where Jesus says,

"Not everyone who says to Me, 'Lord, Lord,' will enter the kingdom of heaven, but he who does the will of My Father who is in heaven will enter. Many will say to Me on that day, 'Lord, Lord, did we not prophesy in Your name, and in Your name cast out demons, and in Your name perform many miracles?' And then I will declare to them, '**I never knew you; depart from me, you who practice lawlessness**" (Matthew 7:21-23)

Those who stand in front of Jesus think they know Him. They *believe* they have met all the requirements for entrance into eternal life, but Jesus says they are dead wrong. Jesus says he doesn't even *know* them! Just as I made a life and death decision regarding the life of my coworker based on wrong information, they must have based their belief about what it takes to be right with God on incorrect information.

Are you known?

So we have to ask, what does it mean to be "known" by Jesus? I would say the answer to this question is probably the most important one we will ever need to know. If we get the answer wrong, we may be the one standing before Jesus one day when He looks us in the eye and says "I never knew you, depart from me." In this passage, those who stood before Him thought they knew Him and literally staked their lives on it. So, this really is a life and death question.

As they stood before Jesus, in an effort to defend themselves, they were listing off things they *thought were evidence* of knowing Jesus. If that was you or me today, we might list some things like the following.

- I attended Church regularly.
- I put my kids in Christian schools so they would learn about God.
- I sang in the Church choir.
- I read my Bible daily, well ...ok; I read a devotional now and then.
- I studied the Bible so I could defend you.
- I gave to the Church building fund.
- I volunteered in the childcare ministry (and even changed diapers!) etc. etc. etc.

All the things that the "average" American Church attendee might come up with don't compare to their list. They mention speaking prophesy, casting out demons and working miracles in the name of Jesus! All things that we would typically associate with the power of God; things done by God "through" a godly person in the power of the Holy Spirit! Notice, Jesus didn't say "Stop lying! You never did these things!" He said, "I never *knew* you, depart from me, **you who practice lawlessness.**"

What is lawlessness?

And that brings up the question, what is lawlessness and what does "practicing lawlessness" mean? How can these followers be doing the things of God, all the while looking the part a Spirit-filled Christian, yet Jesus considers them practitioners of "lawlessness"? In light of the above verse, whatever this lawlessness is, it is a barrier to knowing Jesus and is *evidence* of a lack of relationship and being known by Him. *Lawlessness is the evidence Jesus points to as* **proof** *of his not knowing these people who think they are right with God, but aren't.* So what is lawlessness? The Apostle John lets us know exactly what it is in 1 John 3:4,

"Everyone who sins breaks the law; in fact, ***sin is lawlessness.***"

If sinning *is* lawlessness, then those standing before Jesus who are *practicing sin* must be living as though, and believing, that the law doesn't apply to them. How else could they believe they were in a right standing and relationship with Jesus? Yet Jesus points to this lawlessness (breaking the law, sinning) as the very proof that he doesn't know them. If we look at this verse in context of the surrounding verses, we will get a clearer picture of what the Apostle John is saying to his fellow Christians. Note, he is not speaking those who have rejected Christ; he is speaking to those who claim to be *believers*.

"...when Christ appears, we shall be like him, for we shall see Him as He is. All who have this hope in Him *purify themselves*, just as He is pure. Everyone who sins breaks the law; in fact, sin is lawlessness. But you know that He appeared so that He might take away our sins. And in Him is no sin. ***No one who lives in Him keeps on sinning***. ***No one who continues to sin has either seen Him or known Him. Dear children, do not let anyone*** *lead you astray.* The one who does what is right is righteous, just as He is righteous. The one who does what is sinful is of the devil, because the devil has been sinning from the beginning. The reason the Son of God appeared was to destroy the devil's work. No one who is born of God will continue to sin, because God's seed remains in them; **they cannot go on sinning, because they have been born of God.** *(v. 4-8)*

During all my years as a Christian, I had been consistently taught about freedom from the *consequence* of sin, but rarely had I been taught that I could, should or even *needed* to be free *from* sinning. As a result, I never realized that I should have any part in overcoming the sin in my life. If you have had the same experience, I know that these verses can be a shock to your spiritual underpinning if not understood correctly.

"You never know how much you really believe anything until its truth or falsehood becomes a matter of life and death to you."

~ C.S. Lewis ~

If you will persevere in understanding this, you will come to understand that we are justified by faith in a single moment. However, our sanctification by faith is progressive and ongoing and ***is the evidence*** that the seed of the Gospel has taken root in us, producing the fruit of the Spirit. Said another way, the growing fruit of the Spirit is evidence that we have been justified by faith. The growth of spiritual fruit takes time and seasons so we can't expect full, mature fruit immediately, but if there is no fruit *in process* we need to be concerned.

I want to make clear how much Christ loves us. We who have been trapped in sexual sin have the enemy constantly whispering in our ear about the failures of our lives, telling us that we are unlovable, unforgivable and shaming us. See these for the lies that they are. Christ died for you and couldn't love you more! But we also need to see clearly what He bought for us. It is not just forgiveness (as amazing as that is) but it is also freedom and power to overcome bondage to sin. You need to know God loves you but He also expects you to fight against sin and unbelief as evidence of your faith. So, reject any condemnation you might feel and receive this word as encouragement from God that there is freedom!

Freedom from the law

I used to tell myself any conviction I felt over continued sin in my life was just Satan trying to get me to doubt my salvation. In order to justify my sin, I used a tactic you probably use. I would quote the Bible to myself, saying, "The Bible says we are free from the law and there is no condemnation for those who are in Christ Jesus."

There is great truth in these verses, but that truth is not that we have freedom to continue walking in the flesh and *practicing* sin. This is addressed by Paul in

Romans 8 at length, but his disciple, Timothy states it more succinctly,

"But we know that the Law is good, if one uses it lawfully, realizing the fact that *law is not made for a righteous person, but for those who are lawless* and... for the unholy... immoral men ...according to the glorious gospel of the blessed God..." (1 Timothy 1:8-11)

John is saying (1 John 3:4) that the person who keeps on sinning is lawless and continues to break the law. Timothy is saying that those who are lawless are under the law! I don't think it is a stretch to believe that those standing before Jesus in Matthew 7 believed that they could continue to sin (living in lawlessness) because the law no longer applied to them. They misunderstood grace, believing that they could indulge in sin without consequence and were deceived into thinking they were in right relationship with God! Could this be? Isn't this the belief and perception that is walked out in the life of most American Christians today?

How is it then that the Apostle Paul can say we are no longer under the law but under grace? Are we misunderstanding the true meaning of this verse we often hang our eternal destinies on?

Does grace remove the law?

The book of Romans is an exciting book that deals with answers to these kinds of questions. Dealing with sin directly is not a very popular topic in the American Church, so relatively few preachers teach on it. However, here is what Paul says in Romans chapter 8.

"Therefore, there is now no condemnation (sentence of death) for those who are in Christ Jesus, because through Christ Jesus the *law of the Spirit* who gives life has set you free from the *law of sin and death.*" (v. 1, 2)

Paul says that the removal of our death sentence brought by Jesus comes through the "law of the Spirit" which frees us from the "law of sin and death." If we are in Christ we, *are* free from the law...of sin and death, but we are now subject to the law of the Spirit. We cannot operate under both or neither! Jesus said "You cannot serve two masters...you will be devoted to one and despise the other" (Matthew 6:24). Paul continues....

"For what the law *(of sin and death)* was powerless to do... God did by sending his own Son in the likeness of sinful flesh to be a sin offering. And so He condemned sin ...*in order that the righteous requirement of the law might be fully met in us, who do not live according to the flesh but according to the Spirit.*" (v. 3, 4)

What!? The requirement of the law might be met *in* us - by not walking in the flesh but according to the Spirit? What does that mean? Paul goes on.

"Those who live according to the flesh have their minds set on what the flesh desires; but those who live in accordance with the Spirit have their minds set on what the Spirit desires." (v. 6)

If our minds are set on fleshly desires (lusts), then we are under the law of sin and death; if our minds are set on what the Spirit of God desires then we are under the law of the Spirit.

"The mind governed by the flesh is death, but the mind governed by the Spirit is life and peace. The mind governed by the flesh is hostile to God; it does not submit to God's law, nor can it do so." (v. 6, 7)

The clear implication is that *if* we are not operating under the law of the Spirit, we are operating under the law of sin and death and unable to submit to God's law. We are considered "hostile" towards God. However, if we are operating under the law of the Spirit of life, we can submit to God's law (keep the law) through the power of the Holy Spirit and fully meet the righteous requirement of the law!

Fulfilling the law

If you have been a Christian for any length of time, you know the requirements of the "law of sin and death". It can be summarized this way; if you commit any sin, you are subject to the penalty of eternal punishment. So, what is this "law of the Spirit of life" and how does it work? Galatians 5 provides the answer.

"For the *entire law is fulfilled in keeping this one command*: 'Love your neighbor as yourself.'...So I say, walk by the Spirit, and you *will not* gratify the desires of the flesh. For the flesh desires what is contrary to the Spirit and the Spirit what is contrary to the flesh. They are in conflict with each other... But *if you are led by the Spirit, you are not under the law*", (the law of sin and death). (v. 13-18)

Paul goes on to identify what walking in the flesh looks like.

"The acts of the flesh are obvious: sexual immorality, impurity and debauchery; idolatry and witchcraft; hatred, discord, jealousy, fits of rage, selfish ambition, dissensions, factions and envy; drunkenness, orgies, and the like. *I warn you, as I did before, that those who live like this will not inherit the kingdom of God.*" (v. 19-21)

Yikes, that last sentence should get our attention! He then identifies what walking in the Spirit is.

"...but the fruit of the Spirit is love, joy, peace, forbearance, kindness, goodness, faithfulness, gentleness and *self-control*. Against such things there is no law. *Those who belong to Christ Jesus have crucified the flesh with its passions and desires.*" (v. 22-25)

If we walk according to the Spirit, we come out from being in subjection to the law of sin and death and are under the law of the Spirit of life. In doing so, the requirement of the law is met *in us, not in our own effort, but by our participation with the Holy Spirit*. If we walk according to the Spirit we will produce the fruit of the Spirit in keeping with the one command that Paul said fulfills the law, "Love your neighbor as yourself."

The grace of God is meant to supply forgiveness for the sins we committed prior to our surrender to Christ and for all of the sins we commit in the process of taking down the giants in our life as we daily yield in obedience to our savior. If there is no fight to take down the giants and we willfully choose sin, believing it doesn't matter because we once parroted a prayer ...we are in dangerous trouble.

"If we *deliberately continue sinning* (choice is involved) after we have received the knowledge of the truth, no sacrifice for sin is left." (Hebrews 10.26)

Chapter 11 | What do you know?

"Get Real" Questions for discussion with other men:

If you were standing before Jesus right now, is there any chance He would say, you are one who "practices" sin?

Do you know you are saved? Is your belief based on the studied word of God or what someone told you? What is the evidence?

Can you explain differences of the Law of Sin and Death vs. the Law of the Spirit?

How has this chapter changed your view of sin that is not dealt with decisively in the life of a Christian?

Chapter 12 | Jesus shares a secret

Overcoming sin, blessed though it surely is, is but the bare minimum of a believer's experience. There is nothing astonishing in it. Not to overcome sin is what ought to astonish us."[1]

"Likewise, every good tree bears good fruit, but a bad tree bears bad fruit." (Matthew 7:17)

"Let us not become weary in doing good, for at the proper time we will reap a harvest if we do not give up." (Galatians 6:9)

Matthew chapter 13 tells us that one day as Jesus was sitting by the lake, the people came to hear his teaching and He told them a parable of the good news, the gospel. Here is what He said,

"A farmer went out to sow his seed. As he was scattering the seed, some fell along the path, and the birds came and ate it up. Some fell on rocky places, where it did not have much soil. It sprang up quickly, because the soil was shallow. But when the sun came up, the plants were scorched, and they withered because they had no root. Other seed fell among thorns, which grew up and choked the plants. Still other seed fell on good soil, where it produced a crop—a hundred, sixty or thirty times what was sown. He who has ears, let him hear."

The disciples didn't understand and later, when alone with Jesus, they asked why He spoke in parables, looking for an explanation. Before Jesus answers them, He makes a very interesting statement. *"The knowledge of the secrets of the kingdom of heaven has been given to you, but not to them."* Then He explains.

"Listen then to what the parable of the sower means: When anyone hears the message about the kingdom and does not understand it, the evil one comes and snatches away what was sown in his heart. This is the seed sown along the path. The one who received the seed that fell on rocky places is the man who hears the word and at once *receives* it with joy. But since he has no root, he lasts only a short time. When trouble or persecution comes because of the word, he quickly falls away. The one who *received* the seed that fell among the thorns is the man who hears the word, but the worries of this life and the deceitfulness of wealth choke it, making it *unfruitful.* But the one who *received* the seed that fell on good soil is the man who hears the word and understands it. He *produces a crop*, yielding a hundred, sixty or thirty times what was sown."

We can harvest a few things from this text. First, notice that there are four types of soils mentioned; along the path, the rocky soil, the soil among the thorns, and the good soil. Second, the seed is the good news, the gospel message. Third, the "seed" is sown by a farmer who expects a crop. That is why the seed is sown. In fact, in describing the soil among the thorns, specific mention is made that the ground was "unfruitful" compared to the good ground, which yielded a bountiful crop. The ultimate goal of the farmer is a crop, fruitfulness. The Gospel is meant to produce Christlikeness in your life and that means dominion over sin.

What I think is important to point out is that three of the four soils, 75% of the hearers in this parable, received the seed, the gospel message, and it took root and *began* to grow in their life. However, only one of the three soils produced a crop. The evidence that the kingdom of God has truly taken effect in the life of the receiver is not the seed taking root, but rather, the bearing of fruit. The clear warning in this parable, the secret that Jesus was sharing is that *there is more to entering the kingdom than receiving the gospel message*. A person can receive the gospel message and the message can germinate and begin to grow in a person's life, but it will never meet God's expectation if it does not produce the intended crop! A person may receive the message, and by all outward appearances look "leafy," but never mature to the point of actually producing fruit. In this parable those who dont bear fruit ultimately die! There is no harvest without fruit.

Holiness is what we need

Although the primary topic of this book is addressing sexual sin, it isn't necessarily only about this type of sin. I focused on sexual sin because of the unbelievable and growing level of sexual bondage in the Church. Most men struggle with the various forms of lust and recognize this as a stronghold in their lives and so I address it. This book is really about holiness, and all sin keeps us from the holiness that God requires.

> *"No evil dooms us hopelessly except the evil we love, and desire to continue in, and make no effort to escape from."*
>
> ~ George Elliott ~

For me, this recognition of the vacuum of holiness in the Church came from the understanding that my own sexual sin was a huge barrier to a real relationship and intimacy with Christ. Hebrews Chapter 6 is another passage that speaks directly to us today about the urgency of this issue,

"Therefore let us leave the *elementary teachings* about Christ and go on to maturity, not laying again the **foundation of repentance from acts that lead to death**, and of faith in God. Instruction about baptisms, the laying on of hands, the resurrection of the dead, and eternal judgment. And God permitting, we will do so." (Hebrews 6:1-3)

Repentance from acts that lead to death (sexual sin) is an elementary teaching. Many of us embrace sexual sin repeatedly, relying on the hope that all we need to do is *say* words of repentance while never dealing with the heart issue. We fall into this destructive spiral of sin and repentance, never producing any real fruit of the Spirit. This is not how God intended for us to walk.

"It is impossible for those who have once been enlightened, who have tasted the heavenly gift, who have shared in the Holy Spirit, who have tasted the goodness of the word of God and the powers of the coming age *if they fall away*, to be brought back to repentance, because to their loss they are crucifying the Son of God all over again and subjecting Him to public disgrace." (v. 4-6)

According to my lexicon, the phrase "If they fall away" means "to deviate from the right path, wander" or "fall away from the worship of the true God." We have already established that sexual sin in all its forms is idol worship, and a deviation from worshiping our God and looking to other "gods" to meet our needs. Our relying on grace under the guise of repentance is a deadly game and can only be played by "Christians" who are blind to spiritual realties. Even a fleeting glimpse of the holiness Christ bought for us should cause us to cling to the feet of Jesus in adoration and worship, and seek to obey Him out of heart felt love.

"Land that drinks in the rain often falling on it and that produces a crop useful to those for whom it is farmed receives the blessing of God. *But land that produces thorns and thistles is worthless and is in danger of being cursed. **In the end it will be burned.**"* (v. 6-8)

According to Jesus' parable of the soils, it is not a contradiction for a person to receive the gospel, have it take root in them, then never yield the fruit required for the harvest intended. The writer to the Hebrews confirms this same thought. Here the believer is likened to land that drinks the water, receives the rain from God, and has tasted of his goodness and sharing in the Holy Spirit, yet falls away, producing weeds rather than fruit. Those who worship idols (sex sin in all its forms) are among those who have wandered away from the true worship of God and are equated to soil that does not yield the required harvest, just like the soils mentioned in Matthew 7!

Another parable that confirms this is taught by Jesus in Matthew 13, called the parable of the weeds,

"The kingdom of heaven is like a man who sowed good seed in his field. But while everyone was sleeping, his enemy came and sowed weeds among the wheat, and went away. When the wheat sprouted and formed heads, then the weeds also appeared. The owner's servants came to Him and said, 'Sir, didn't you sow good seed in your field? Where then did the weeds come from?' "'An enemy did this,' he replied. "The servants asked Him, 'Do you want us to go and pull them up?' "'No,' he answered, 'because while you are pulling the weeds, you may uproot the wheat with them. Let both grow together until the harvest. At that time I will tell the harvesters: First collect the weeds and tie them in bundles to be burned; then gather the wheat and bring it into my barn." (Matthew 13:24-30)

I was fortunate to grow up in the farm country of Oregon. Our neighbor farmed multiple crops and one of them was wheat; in fact, the field right next to our house was a large wheat field. You could see it from almost every room in the house. What is interesting about wheat is that as it sprouts and grows it looks very much like common field grass. It would be nearly impossible to discern and remove the actual grass from the wheat sprouts as they begin to grow, but as the wheat matures it begins to produce a head. Some of the field grass does as well, but there are subtle differences to someone who knows wheat. As the wheat approaches maturity there comes a point where you are clearly able to distinguish between the grass and the wheat, and at full maturity, the clear and obvious differentiation is the "fruit," the full head of grain. At this maturity, there is no mistaking the wheat from the weeds. In this parable, the "fruit' is what God identifies as the difference between those who are harvested and those who are gathered and burned.

Seeing Clearly

A while back I bought a new car, a Volkswagen Beetle. All of a sudden everywhere I looked there were Volkswagen Beetles! As God opened my eyes and I dealt with my own sexual sin, I began to see how much, how often, and how bluntly the Bible warns us that sexual sin will keep us from a relationship with God, and lives that produce the fruit of the Spirit. It has become clear to me that the staggering numbers of the men who sit in Church each week, snared by sexual sin and the resulting devastation to marriages and families, break the heart of God.

I imagine right now many of you are somewhat stunned by the implication of what this chapter may mean for you if you are still embracing sexual sin in your life. I want to make clear one more time that this book is not meant to bring condemnation on anyone. Conviction yes, but also to point you to the grace of God that provides not just forgiveness, but *freedom* from the bondage of sin. God provides a way for us to overcome the sin in our lives. Just as the enemy used us as willing participant to break the heart of God, God requires our willing participation in overcoming the sin in our lives. Unfortunately, most of us haven't been taught this.

The Gospel has two sides

The Gospel has two sides, side one is Justification: Jesus, the messiah, God, loved you so much that He came to earth, suffered and died to take the punishment for your sin upon Himself. (John 3:16) If you believe in your heart this is true, and acknowledge Him as Lord God and Savior of your life, confessing this with your mouth, you will receive eternal life. (Romans 10:9) Justification cleans the slate and places us in right standing with God.

Most of American evangelism focuses on getting people to repeat a prayer, and many believers consider this the finish line. "I got my ticket for the train to heaven. I'm in! Now I can rest easy. The fire insurance policy is in place and paid in full!"

My mother used to always quote to me,

"You believe that there is one God. Good! Even the demons believe that, and shudder." (James 2:19)

I didn't understand at the time what she was getting at (or maybe I didn't want to) but now I think I do. There is something implied in the word *believe* as James uses it that is very different from what most Christians understand, something beyond intellectual acknowledgment. When the Israelites were wandering the desert, if we were to ask them if they believed God was real and that he delivered them from Egypt, parted the Red Sea and provided manna from heaven for them, they surely would have said yes. They believed in God.

Their belief, however, was passive. The initial decision for them was, "do we stay in Egypt as slaves of Pharaoh or allow Moses to lead us out of here to a land of milk and honey?" For many of us, the initial decision for Christ was a result of answering the question, "Do I want to go to heaven or hell when I die?" Hmm, when we put it that way it seems like a no-brainer, but, there is a process that is required to take place to complete the journey. Getting out of Egypt was necessary but it isn't the finish line, it is only the beginning.

Side two of the Gospel is Sanctification: When the Israelites came to Kadesh Barnea, on the edge of the Promised Land, God asked for their active belief. A belief that was willing to stake the continued life of the nation on action in obedience to God. He asked them to fight the giants in the land, trusting that He would fight for and through them. When they refused, God was so angry that He told Moses He wanted to destroy them for their lack of belief. (Numbers 14) There is a difference between passive and active belief, and God *requires* active belief from us. To get a clearer understanding, look at James 2 in this context.

"What does it profit, my brethren, if someone says he has faith (belief) but does not have works (active obedience)? Can faith (belief) save him? ... faith (belief) by itself, if it does not have works (active obedience), *is dead*... You believe that there is one God. You do well. Even the demons believe (mental acknowledgment) — and tremble! But do you want to know, *O foolish man*, that faith (belief) without works (active obedience) is dead? Was not Abraham our father justified by works (active obedience) when he offered Isaac his son on the altar? Do you see that faith (belief) was working together with his works (active obedience), and by works (active obedience) faith (belief) was made perfect? And he was called the friend of God. *You see then that a man is justified by works (active obedience), and not by faith (belief) only.*

I want to make clear; we cannot earn our place in heaven. Active obedience is done out of love to God and his word and is evidence of the process of sanctification, the transforming our hearts into Christ likeness. It is the evidence that we are truly God's children in relationship with Him. I want to emphasize the transforming of the heart into Christ likeness because, as mentioned earlier, it is possible to do the "right things" externally, looking the part without any heart change. The external action may not be motivated out of love for God and hatred of sin, but rather from the motives of the flesh; acclaim, acknowledgment, vanity, guilt, trying to "earn" God's approval etc.

The transformation of the heart can only take place in relationship to Christ and that is why Jesus could say "I never knew you." Even though those standing before Him had done great works in his name, there was never an active obedience that dealt with the condition, the sinfulness of a heart, so as to be conformed into Christ likeness.

A transformed heart cannot happen if we are content to remain in a state of passive belief. Remaining in passive belief is a state where sin continues to reign in our lives. A place where we are content to wallow in our sin, believing that God will not, or cannot conquer the sins in our lives. Or, that He expects us to do it in our own power and effort which is impossible.

"Heart-suffering because of sin is the best proof that the Holy Spirit dwells in your heart"

~Johann Arndt ~

Many want God, like a genie, to deliver us, but God says, just as He did to the Israelite's at Kadesh Barnea, "I will deliver the giants into your hands but you must fight!" We cannot do it on our own and God will not do it without us! This is the process of becoming holy and it only happens in relationship and obedience to God.

This is not because God can't do it without our help, He can, and occasionally does surprise us with his special grace in this way, but his typical pattern is to require our human will to participate in active obedience with his Holy Spirit in eradicating sin from our lives. In the process, our relationship with him develops in a way that would never happen if, like a genie in bottle, He removed every obstacle for us without any active belief and expressed faith on our part.

In addition, the fight for faith in the heat of the battle grows our spiritual character and strengthens our ability to trust him ever more deeply as we conquer the sin in our lives.

Romans 5:3-4 says, "...we also rejoice in our sufferings, because we know that suffering (applied pressure) produces perseverance; perseverance, character (proved character)..."

As New Testament believers, we are called in active obedience to deal with the giants in our lives, the sin that seeks to control us. Living in side one of the Gospel is a Gospel that keeps us endlessly wandering in the desert. It was never meant to be our destination. It is only a staging ground where the fundamental lessons of faith and obedience toward God are learned for entry into the Spirit-filled life of warfare on sin. With victory over sin comes the peace and rest we seek.

Side two is evidence that the Kingdom of heaven spoken of by Jesus is in you, and is proof that the Spirit of God is working in your life. I can hear many of you resisting what I am sharing. Passive belief is so much easier than active belief. Who wants to fight giants if you don't have to, and especially the giant of sexual sin? Everything in us wants to just fall on the grace of God and believe we are "in." We prefer to believe that unless

God does a miracle for us, we will struggle with this sin all our lives, but God says this is a battle we *must* fight.

Hebrews 12.14 says, "Make every effort (re-read Matthew 5:27-30, get drastic!) ...to be holy; *without holiness no one will see the Lord*...See that no one is sexually immoral, or is godless like Esau, who for a single meal sold his inheritance rights as the oldest son..."

The writer of the letter to the Ephesians says,

"...Christ loved the Church and gave himself up for her to make her holy, cleansing her by the washing with water through the word, and to present her to Himself as a radiant Church, *without stain or wrinkle or any other blemish, but holy and blameless.*"

If 60 percent of the men in the Church are addicted to porn, then we are not the Church that Christ expects to be presented to Him as his bride. You may be tempted to say, well, we are considered holy already by Christ's payment for our sin. We have already addressed this; James says that a faith that has no active obedience is a dead faith. So does God really expect us to live in victory over sexual sin in our lives?

Yes.

"For this is the will of God, your sanctification (pursuit of holiness): that you abstain from sexual immorality; that each one of you know how to control his own body in holiness and honor, not in the passion of lust like the Gentiles who do not know God." (1 Thessalonians 4:3-5)

Chapter 12 | Jesus shares a secret

"Get Real" Questions for discussion with other men:

What are your thoughts about the four soils mentioned by Jesus and the land mentioned in Hebrews as it relates to your life?

What is the difference between Justification and Sanctification? Can you have one without the other? How do you know if either is working in your life?

What is your reaction to God requiring our active participation in killing our personal sin giants?

Reread Hebrews 12:14. Why do you think the writer equated sexual sin with Esau selling his inheritance for a single meal? Why do you think he made a point of letting us know that Esau was unable to get his inheritance back?

Do you see God's will as stated in 1 Thessalonians 4:3-5 as possible in modern America?

Chapter 13 | Is it in you?

"The inner change, justification, is effected at the moment of salvation. The outer change in the believer's daily walk, sanctification, continues throughout life. But the progressive work of sanctification is only fully effective when the radical, inner transformation of justification is realized and appropriated by faith." [1]

"But you will receive power when the Holy Spirit comes upon you and you will be my witnesses..." (Acts 1:8)

John was the product of divorce. He grew up without ever knowing his father. He only knew what his mother told him about being a man, and that wasn't a lot. As a result, he pretty much made up the "manhood rules" as he went along. He gained most of his measure of morality from the media and culture around him. It was pretty much his to pick and choose what it meant to be a man.

John was one of those guys who always pushed the boundaries. In school, it seemed the rules didn't apply to him. He wasn't blatant about it, but he dabbled in drugs, experimented sexually with the girls and never experienced any serious negative effects. He never got addicted to anything and no one ever got pregnant, at least not that he knew of. When he did have a close call due to cutting some moral corner or found himself in a pinch, he could rely on his quick charm and winning smile to talk his way of any serious consequences.

After college he got married to his sweetheart, Sara. Neither of them had good jobs yet, but they did have credit cards which paid for the honeymoon, and they spared no expense. When they got back from the honeymoon, it wasn't long before they both had good entry level jobs. Soon John used his charm and a little deceit on the loan application to get them into a home with an adjustable-rate mortgage. He took a cash advance on the credit cards for the down payment but hid that from the bank. They used the credit cards again for all the new furnishings they needed. Offers for additional credit cards with healthy dollar limits continued to come in the mail every so often. They signed up for all of them; after all, you want to keep your financial options open in case you get in trouble or need some quick cash!

John and Sara never really exercised any discipline or restraint when it came to buying or doing whatever they desired. There was no need, after all, credit was easy to come by and interest rates were relatively low. New clothes, nice cars, vacations, any pleasure or comfort they desired. Whatever it was, they simply put it on the credit cards, banking that there would be future raises, bonuses and more credit if needed.

After a decade John decided to start his own business and the bank wouldn't loan him the start up cash due to their large debt. However, he didn't let that stop him, he maxed out the credit cards with cash advances and plunged forward.

Well, the business didn't take off as quickly as planned and the economy began slowing down. Between the two of them, they were just able to keep their heads above water financially, but it was beginning to create stress and strain on their relationship. They could no longer keep up the lifestyle they had been living. That's when Sara got laid off in the downsizing, and shortly afterward they found out Sara was pregnant… with twins!

Very quickly, they realized they were in desperate trouble, and paying the debt they had accumulated was like trying to swim with an anchor tied around their neck. The economy was in the toilet, his business was failing, Sara was about to have two babies, and it wouldn't be long before they would be homeless and destitute if a miracle didn't happen. And it did.

Through a series of amazing "coincidences," John happened to learn that the father he never knew was looking for him and his father happened to be wealthy beyond anything John could imagine.

As John and his father established their new relationship, John shared the predicament he and Sara had gotten themselves into, telling his father how desperate they were. John's father immediately agreed to pay off all of their debt, saving them from financial ruin. It truly was a miracle! To make it even more amazing, his father gave him signatory power to access his unlimited corporate credit line so that he and Sara could partake in whatever pleasure, indulgences or creature comforts their hearts desired. Debt would never be a problem again. It was easy street from now on!

Debt Free

You've probably figured out that the story of John and Sara is fictitious. Substitute "sin" for "debt" in this story and you have an example of how the majority of American Christian men approach sexual sin and God's grace. Because our typical experience is that we are unable to overcome our sin in our own effort, we embrace a theology that says we don't need to. We have an unlimited credit line; not only for our past sins, but also for any future sin we choose to embrace.

When Jesus died and rose again he said in John 16:7,

"...I tell you the truth: it is to your advantage that I go away, for if I don't go away the counselor won't come to you. But if I go, I will send him to you."

And in Acts 1:8,

"But you will receive power when the Holy Spirit comes upon you and you will be my witnesses..."

On our own, we have gotten ourselves desperately into sin debt, and our Father in heaven sent Jesus to pay the sin debt on our behalf; but not so that we will have the freedom to continue racking up sin debt without limit or consequence for the remainder of our lives. In fact, just the opposite. He sent the sin debt counselor, the Holy Spirit, *not just to guide us, but to live in us* to keep us out of sin debt.

Our credit line for the payment of sin is intended for sin we stumble into in the process of becoming increasingly more like Christ. It was never intended to cover the sin we wantonly seek out and practice! In fact, if the Holy Spirit lives within us, the only way we can knowingly choose to sin is to *willfully ignore* the counselor that Jesus said would be of more benefit to us than his personal presence.

> "Men do not differ much about what things they call evil; they differ enormously about what evils they will call excusable."
>
> ~ G. K. Chesterton ~

A witness for Christ

I spend a bit of time at the gym working off the stresses of daily life and trying to keep the weeds from taking the garden of my aging body. Here is an example I can relate to, and I hope you can too. Let's say, just for sake of illustration, that you have 20 extra pounds you would like to lose. I am sure that is not the case, but just humor me.

Can you imagine this scenario? You have just been notified of an incredible deal for a series of sessions at the local gym that includes a one on one meeting with a personal trainer each week for the next ten weeks. The trainer will measure your body fat composition, work with you and a nutritionist to develop a customized diet plan, and then set up a workout and exercise plan *guaranteeing* you will easily lose an extra 20 pounds over the ten week schedule.

Wow! Sounds great! You schedule the appointment in great anticipation. About a week later, you show up at the health club for your first meeting. Your wait isn't long before a kind-looking young man about 28 years old and about 60 lbs. overweight approaches you with his hand out. He smells faintly of having just come back from a "smoke" break. You quickly size him up; "*Ah yes,*" you think to yourself, "*this is where I get the sales pitch for the gym membership*" and you ready your resolve to resist being sold. As you reach out to shake his hand he introduces himself as Toby, your new personal trainer!

Now, I don't know about you, but I have never been able to give much credibility to people who live "do as I say, not as I do" lives. If I am going to allow someone to teach me, give me advice, or tell me how to be successful at something, especially if I am paying money for their expertise, I expect them to have applied the information to their own lives. I want my personal trainer to look the part of a personal trainer, one who has actually practiced what he is about to teach me.

In looking at Toby my thoughts would be, "*either Toby doesn't live by the principles he is going to share with me or he isn't motivated to live by them. If he isn't motivated to live them, how is he going to relate to the mental challenges I am going to face? How is he going to encourage me to persevere when discouragement and temptation strike? Looking at his success surely doesn't motivate me!* He will have little credibility with me, and I will give little weight to what he says about the necessity and benefits of nutrition and exercise because he isn't living the life.

This is the same situation most Christians face when proclaiming our faith in Jesus, exhorting others to join us. We in essence say, "do as I say, not as I do," and when that is the case, we have no credibility and the world mocks both us and Jesus.

The Holy Spirit was given to us for the express purpose of being witnesses of the love *and* power of Christ (Acts 1:8). The modern American Church has generally interpreted this to mean that we need to get out of our comfort zone and communicate the plan of salvation to unbelievers. We typically do this by encouraging the "un-Churched" at every opportunity to say a prayer and adhere to the Christian do's and don'ts for a new standard of living. If we do this while refusing to deal with our own hidden sin, the world sees us as hypocrites, trying to hold the world to a standard we don't keep ourselves.

We tend to condemn the sexual sin of the world but excuse our own sexual sin under the banner of grace! Let me approach this from another direction in the extreme with a question. Consider a practicing pedophile that says a prayer, acknowledging Christ as savior and then goes on molesting children, making no effort to change. Would you consider this person to be a biblical example of the transforming power of God as he witnesses to others about the power of Christ? You would say no, because there has been no true repentance and lifestyle change. Yet, this is exactly what much of the Church does in regard to our own sexual sin. We claim to serve a God who has birthed a new life in us but there is no true evidence of a new life in inward or outward demonstration. We have a form of Godliness but no power to live the life we claim to have.

The Apostle Paul said,

"Follow my example, as I follow Christ" (1 Corinthians 11:1)

Few Christians can say this. Our Christian witness is apathetic and weak, and the Church is riddled with divorce and sexual sin. The Church in general is not walking in the power of the Holy Spirit and we are mostly blind to the fact, thinking we are in right standing with God. If our pastors are aware of unconfronted sin in the Church, few are willing to address it for fear of offending the "seeker" in our midst. In our dumbing down of the full gospel message for fear of offending, we in essence continue to lower the call to holiness and may be building Churches filled with people who, in reality, have no saving relationship with Jesus.

Where are you?

Here are a few questions for you to ponder as you assess and examine our own relationship with Christ. They will help you determine whether the Gospel has truly taken root in you and your salvation is true. These come from Pastor John Piper.[2]

1) *By the Holy Spirit we cry "Abba" Father. The Spirit Himself testifies with our spirit that we are God's children"* (Romans 8:15-16)

- Does your spirit cry out to God as your papa father or is He a distant authoritarian?

- Do you have a deep awareness that the Spirit of God dwells in you and is your "helper," and the connection that allows you to communicate intimately with your father in heaven?

- Do you have a peaceful sense that God loves you so much that He longs to meet with you every day?

2) *The natural man does not welcome the things of the Spirit of God, for they are foolishness (and unimportant) to him* (1 Corinthians 2:14).

- Do you crave the things of God?

- Do you long to spend time alone with Him each day?

- Is your relationship with God a priority in your daily routine?

- If you pursue Him in prayer and Godly disciplines, is it out of desire or duty?

- Are your highest priorities eternal, or are they worldly comfort and pleasure?

- Does your spending reflect that your highest priorities are eternal?

3) *God chose you to be saved through the sanctifying work of the Holy Spirit and through belief in the truth.* (2 Thessalonians 2:13)

- Are you walking in the flesh or the Spirit?
- Are you having progressive victory over sin in your life?
- Are you progressing in producing the fruit of the Spirit daily?
- Are the desires of your heart moving away from sin toward God?
- Does your sin cause you pain?

The answers to these questions deserve deep consideration, and if needed, repentance and a prayerful conversation with your savior because one day each of us will stand before Christ He will say one of two things.

"I never knew you; depart from me, you who practice lawlessness (sin)" (Matthew 7:23) Or will He say,

"Well done, good and faithful servant, come and share your master's happiness." (Matthew 25:23)

Meant to shine

Our witness as Christian men is not meant to be in word only. When the Spirit of God indwells us there should be a radical difference in us that is visible to those in the world we interact with. Paul says the following,

"For **we know** brothers and sisters loved by God, **that He has chosen you, because** our gospel came to you not simply with words but also with power, with the Holy Spirit and deep conviction...**you became imitators of us and of the Lord**..." (1 Thessalonians 1:4-6)

Paul is saying that the gospel presented with the Holy Spirit is powerful, enabling us to become Christ-like. In his letter to the Philippians Paul describes us,

"...as children of God without fault in a warped and crooked generation such that we will shine among the sinful like stars in the sky!" (Philippians 2:15)

Dallas Willard in "Hearing God" says it this way:

"Those born of the Spirit manifest a different kind of life...the spiritually born exhibit a life deriving from an invisible spirit realm and its powers. In natural terms one cannot explain what is happening with them, where they come from or where they go (John 3:8). But just as with the invisible wind and its effects, we recognize the presence of God in a person by its effects in and around them."[4]

Preparing for Battle

So where is the power of the gospel to live the life God is calling you to? Why are you not experiencing it? The power comes from the Holy Spirit and He only comes to those who trust in Jesus and are surrendered to Him and welcome Him in. Without the Holy Spirit dwelling in you, there is no power to overcome sin.

When Jesus died on our behalf, He bought back our "will," our ability to "choose." We are no longer slaves in the sense that we have no choice. Just as getting out of monetary debt initially requires us to make choices contrary to our desires until we experience full freedom from the slavery of debt, so it is with slavery to sexual sin. We must choose to obey Christ in opposition to our fleshly desires if we are to escape the pull of sexual sin. It is the Holy Spirit as our counselor that enables us as we walk out this process.

The challenge is listening to and trusting the Holy Spirit. Each day we must surrender our body, soul, mind, spirit, and will to his leading. If we don't, we are open to becoming deaf to his instruction, and falling prey to the counsel of our own minds or that of the enemy. Time with Jesus is the place to start the battle each day.

In the next two chapters I will talk about how this battle is practically fought. To achieve any victory over sin we MUST have an abiding relationship with God. It is the foundation upon which all must be built and is the most important (Matthew 7:24-27). If your battle plan is built on any other foundation it will be unstable and ultimately ineffective. You may gain the world but lose your soul (Matthew 8:36).

Chapter 13 | Is it in you?

"Get Real" Questions for discussion with other men:

In relating to the analogy of John and Sarah, what is the role of the "sin debt counselor" (Holy Spirit) in your life? Is His power evident in your life? In what way?

When the Bible speaks of God as "Abba," Papa, Daddy…is this difficult for you to envision in your relationship to Him. Why?

If we were to look at your life over the last 30 days, what would we see are your highest priorities based on how you spent your time and money? If it is not God, why not?

Are you more like Christ today than a year ago? Would your wife and children agree with you?

Chapter 14 | Enter the battle - Part 1

"In justification the word to be addressed to man is believe – only believe; in sanctification the word must be watch, pray and fight." [1]

"...we do not wage war as the world does. The weapons we fight with are not the weapons of the world. On the contrary, they have divine power to demolish strongholds." (1 Corinthians 10:3-4)

I hope by now that you have come to the realization that we are called to engage in warfare in the name of Christ against the sin in our lives. For most men this has to start with recognizing and dealing with our sinful desires related to sex and lust. However, just like Israel standing on the border of Kadesh Barnea, you have a choice to make that will determine your destiny going forward. There is a line in the sand that you must choose or refuse to cross. That line marks the entry into a new life of victory.

God will not force you into the sanctification process, the pursuit of holiness; instead, He will honor your will. When Israel was under the authority of Pharaoh, they had no freedom to choose. They were slaves, however when standing on the border of the Promised Land, they had a choice to make, the choice to believe God in obedience and fight ...or not.

In accepting Jesus as our savior, we have been delivered from the *authority* of Satan. God has restored to us the freedom to obey. We have the Spirit of God available to us. We have freedom to choose to place our belief in God and his promises or not, however the bible warns us that there are consequences to the choice we make.

Jesus said, "Most assuredly (*here is a truth*), I say to you, anyone who commits sin is a slave to sin" (John 8:34)

The word translated as "commits" can have the meaning of bearing, producing or sprouting forth. I am taking the liberty of relating this to a seed sprouting that, if left to grow, will drive its roots deeper and deeper into the heart and life of the man who refuses to destroy it.

Here is what the Bible says happens to the man who *chooses* to commit sin rather than deal radically with sin in pursuit of holiness.

"Therefore, (as a result) God gave them over in the sinful desires of their hearts to sexual impurity for the degrading of their bodies" (Romans 1:24)

The result of not obeying God and not defeating our sin is that God honors the power of choice that He bought for us through his death on the cross. He allows us to reap the consequence of the sin we embrace. The sexual sin seeds we continue to plant and water begin slowly, almost imperceptibly, to produce a crop, thorns and thistles that choke out the reality of the gospel in our lives. This is how 60 percent of Christian men have become addicted to pornography.

First things first

In Ezekiel chapter 11 God gives Ezekiel a prophesy of his people returning to Him.

"They will return to it (*the land*) and remove all its vile images and detestable idols. I will give them an undivided heart and put a new spirit in them; I will remove from them their heart of stone and give them a heart of flesh." (v. 18, 19)

God indicates that the first order of business, after returning (repentance), is removing the idols from the land! The first step after returning to God and repenting of our sin is to begin to tear down the idols that have taken residence in the soil of our hearts! If we do, God promises to meet us in the process and change our hearts and give us his Spirit!

"Then they will follow my decrees and be careful to keep my laws. They will be my people, and I will be their God" (v. 20)

After God begins the process of transforming our hearts and empowers us by his Spirit, we begin walking in the Spirit, under the law of the Spirit. In us, and through our yielding to the Holy Spirit, the law of God will be fulfilled in us! This is the gospel message in full effect. God goes on to say in verse 21,

"But as for those whose hearts are devoted to their vile images and detestable idols, I will bring down on their own heads what they have done, declares the Sovereign LORD."

> *"God whispers to us in our pleasures, speaks to us in our conscience, but shouts in our pains: It is His megaphone to rouse a deaf world"*
>
> ~C.S. Lewis~

If you, like me, have been seduced into this trap of sexual addiction, I declare to you today there is freedom in Christ. By his amazing love and grace, I have experienced it firsthand. In the remainder of this chapter I will attempt to lay out some practical steps; a battle plan for entering this war for holiness and taking down the giants. These steps are specifically articulated to address the area of sexual sin. It is a pattern of what God has worked in my life and I have seen worked out in the lives of other men.

All these steps are crucial, some more than others, but leaving out or avoiding just one of them *could* be the difference between your success and failure; so I am encouraging you, if you are serious, to go "all in." If you can't make that commitment, consider carefully what a less than an "all in" decision is communicating to the God who went "all in" so you could even have the freedom to make this choice.

If you are ready to return to God, now would be a good time to put this book down and tell God you repent of choosing sin over Him. Tell Him that you "want to want" to walk in holiness but that you *desperately need* his Holy Spirit to change your heart and empower you to trust Him. Ask Him to fill you with his Holy Spirit and power to live for Him. Tell Him you will choose daily to surrender your life, all that you are, to his leading and the word of God, but only if you mean it! Now, let's talk about your first few steps in this battle.

"Get alone with Jesus and either tell Him that you do not want sin to die out in you - or else tell Him that at all costs you want to be identified with His death."

~Oswald Chambers~

Step one – Submit to the Commander in Chief

The first step is to acknowledge and embrace the fact that you cannot defeat your enemy using your own strategies and in your own effort. We have a saying in our men's accountability group that we all come to admit. I think it came from Alcoholics Anonymous. "My own best thinking is what got me to the place I am now." Our own choices and our refusal to give up control have led us to this current place in life.

There is a story I have heard many times about how African hunters will catch a monkey for dinner. As I was writing this, I wondered if it was true. I searched the web and actually found an example on video.[2] I have heard several variations of how this works, but in this particular video, the hunter found what looked like an ant or termite hill in which to construct the trap.

The dirt of the hill was hard like clay and using a stick, the hunter drilled a small cavity into the side of the hill just big enough for the monkey to insert his hand. After he had drilled about four inches into the side of the hill, the back wall of the hole broke through to a wider cavity about five or six inches around. The hunter then took some type of treat and poked it into the narrow hole so that it fell down into the deeper cavity. Then he stepped aside to hide behind some bushes and wait for a curious monkey to venture near. Eventually an unsuspecting monkey comes by, smells the treat and ambles over to investigate. After verifying that there is something yummy in the hole, the monkey reaches in through the narrow opening and grabs the treat, and as he does so he makes a fist.

The hapless monkey is now unable to remove his hand from the hole as long as he holds on to the treat. It is amazing to watch the monkey struggle to get his hand out of the trap while refusing to let go the treat! Even as he sees the hunter walking toward him, he refuses to let go of the treat and make an escape. The monkey frantically howls, twisting this way and that in an effort to keep his treasure as he sees the hunter approaching. In the end, the hunter walks up and easily captures the monkey for a tasty meal.

This little story is loaded with truth and warning for those who think they can hold onto sexual sin and not pay the ultimate price. This monkey refused to let go of his temporary desire and ended up losing his life. We think "Oh, the silly little monkey!" Yet we who love our sin engage in similar thinking, with a bit more subtlety.

We convince ourselves that we have let go of our sin by putting it behind our back and saying words of repentance. We tell God we are his and that we are surrendered to Him, but we keep access to our sin, just in case if we need it. This is not repentance.

In reality, what we are hoping is that God will deliver us without any effort on our part, *then* we will be willing to let go of our sin. We want God to kill the giant without our participation; to take away the desire before we commit to fight, but God does not typically work that way. Our actions say, "God deliver me and then I will obey and have faith." God says "Have faith and obey me, then I will deliver you."

In the epilogue of his book entitled *"The Prayer Life,"* Andrew Murray leaves his readers with this.

"In war, everything depends on each soldier being obedient to the word of command, even though it cost him his life. In our strife with Satan, we will not conquer unless each one of us holds himself ready…to say from the heart 'What God says, I will do and if I see anything according to his will I will immediately receive it and act upon it.' …everything depends upon the spirit of surrender to immediate obedience, according to the word of God."

Submission to God requires a real surrender of our life to his word as our absolute authority, and adherence to his battle plan requires close proximity as his commands and directives for battle are communicated. Of all the decisions you will make in this battle, step 1, true surrender, repentance and regularly meeting with your savior is the most critical. When at war, there *has* to be constant communication between the commander providing direction and those who execute the battle. There *has* to be unquestioned and immediate adherence to the direction of the commander. If not, failure and defeat are just round the corner.

> *"The nature of Christ's salvation is woefully misrepresented by the present-day evangelist. He announces a Savior from Hell rather than a Savior from sin. And that is why so many are fatally deceived, for there are multitudes who wish to escape the Lake of fire who have no desire to be delivered from their carnality and worldliness."*
>
> ~ A.W. Pink ~

Unfortunately, this is where most men seek to cut corners in dealing with sin. They say they are too busy and can't find the time. If this is what you are saying, then in reality, having a relationship with God and defeating your sin isn't a high priority for you. If you are really honest with yourself, you *make* time to do those things you *really want* to do. If it is important *to you*, you *will* find the time. You've been able to find time to engage in sexual sin haven't you...and for how many years?

Jesus stated a truth that allows us to discern the reality of what is important to us, he said,

"Where your treasure is, there will your heart be also" (Matthew 6:21)

For Americans, we have two "treasures" that, in how we spend them reveal the truth about where the desires of our hearts lie. They are money and time. If you tell me that your family is the most important thing in your life but you work 80 hours a week to the neglect of your family, you are deceiving no one. If you tell me that loving others is a high priority and you spend more money on your car payment than you give to charity, again, you deceive no one. If you tell me you have, or want a real, living relationship with God, but you can't make time to get alone with God regularly, you are deceiving no one but yourself.

This again, is a heart issue. Just "doing it" as a matter of duty is not the answer. God doesn't want you going through the motions. He sees right through that. Here is an example I think most guys can relate to. Let's say your wife loves the ballet and you don't like it so much. She comes home and tells you that she just purchased very expensive tickets to go to Swan Lake, and her tone and delivery indicate, without being said directly of course, that she *expects* you to go with her.

As your brilliant mind quickly filters through all the potential responses that might somehow get you off the hook, the painful realization settles in that if you respond in a way viewed as anything but excited about this opportunity, you may not be getting "united" with wife for some time. Wanting to avoid this you bite your tongue and outwardly put on the mask of embracing the event, even though inwardly you would rather watch football.

In the end you go, but your heart is in no way involved. Your motivation was self- serving, selfish. At best, you were operating out of duty in relation to your role as husband, not much different than cleaning the cat box. No joy is involved, and you do it out of obligation.

Here is an alternative. Although you may not utterly enjoy everything about the ballet, you truly are in love with your wife, and you enjoy her company. Your motivation is to be with her and share in the things she enjoys. Your focus is on her and your love for her, not the ballet that you don't enjoy so much. Isn't this precisely what you did you when you first started dating her? You probably would have done just about anything if it meant you could be with her!

God wants a real relationship. We cannot rely on attending Church each Sunday to provide the level of intimate relationship that God wants to have with us. Church has its place, and it may be where we meet with God and other believers each week, but expecting Church to be the place where you get intimate with God is like never meeting with your wife outside of a group date. It can only get so intimate, and there is a level of required (and should be desired) intimacy that just will not take place on a group date.

When we are in love with Jesus, walking in the Spirit isn't a chore. When we adore Him and being in his presence, our desire to please Him and be with Him is greater than our desire to partake in a momentary sin that would be a betrayal of our love for Him. First Corinthians says that if we do all the things that mark us as a Christian but don't have love, it all adds up to a big nothing. It all starts with surrendering to God's battle plan and pursuing a love relationship with Jesus.

Step 2 – Define the battle lines

The next step is as simple and logical as to be assumed however most Christian men never take it. This is one reason why we need other men in our lives that will help us take this step and keep us vigilant in patrolling the boundaries.

We are talking about defining the battle lines and keeping ourselves from "temptation snares" before we stumble or walk into sin. This is a process where you must be honest with yourself and analyze your personal weaknesses. You need to put up barriers to people, places, activities and things that provide temptation, provocation and opportunities to engage in sin. In essence, building a fence around yourself to prevent you from getting into situations where your resolve and commitment to God will fail.

Ultimately, the goal is that you will no longer be tempted to travel these familiar paths. As God changes your heart, situations where you would have eagerly (and easily) fallen to temptation in the past will no longer be a snare to you. As your heart changes, you will begin to see these temptations for what they really are. They may still appeal to the flesh, but the spirit is growing stronger. You will choose to allow those well-worn paths to fade away, however in the short term we need to make sure you stay off the path while the grass grows back!

Depending on your situation, this might include but is not limited to the following types of proactive measures.

- Installing filters on internet access where temptation and opportunity meet.
- Install appropriate filters on phones or tablets with internet access.
- When traveling alone, have adult movies blocked to your room. (Before you arrive!)
- Eliminate access to provocative magazines. (You may need to discontinue going to that convenience store for milk or you might need to tell your wife "no more Victoria's Secret magazines"!)
- Re-evaluate the TV shows and movies you allow yourself to watch.
- Eliminate cable TV, internet access, smart phone, Facebook etc...
- Stop engaging in emotional connections and "harmless" flirting with women you aren't married to. (Waitresses, receptionists etc.)
- Develop clear boundaries for interactions with the opposite sex.

Taking these types of preventive measures are simple and make a lot of sense, however they are rarely easy to do consistently on your own without relying on other men to hold you accountable. There are several reasons why men do not take these simple steps.

One is pride. As long as we don't take these steps, we can avoid admitting to ourselves and others that we have a problem we can't handle by sheer, aggressive willpower. This is difficult for many American men. Admitting that we need God and other men requires humility.

Secondly, and most men view this as the bigger issue, if they are married; a man may fear that his wife will notice the boundary changes he is making and ask what is going on. If your wife isn't aware of the issues Christian men struggle with, and particularly the sexual issues you as her husband are struggling with, there is likely to be fear of condemnation, exposure and rejection if your wife were to find out. This deadly duo of pride and fear is what keeps the majority of Christian men enslaved and addicted. As I have said before, this sin loves to hide, and it just grows stronger and more powerful the longer it goes unexposed.

Defining your initial battle lines requires answering the question, "Based on my past experience, where has the enemy of my soul placed the bait that has caused me to sin against God?" When we first begin to deal with our sexual sin, we tend to define sinful behavior tighter than we had previously, but still more loosely than God does. We may think that if we could just quit looking at porn or end the affair, we will have dealt decisively with our sexual sin. However, as we begin to "take the land" we discover that the sin that brought us to the point of bondage sits atop a foundation of tolerated, smaller sins that paved the way.

Men who are in a true relationship with God and take all the actions necessary to control the boundaries of the battle, eventually realize that a "fence" is not the ultimate answer. The ultimate goal is a renewed mind and a changed heart, not just staying inside the fence. The ultimate goal is to "not want" to go outside the fence, to have our hearts changed and to no longer desire sin.

Our holiness is never a state of perfection or complete sinlessness, but a continual pursuit of Christ-likeness under the armor of God's grace laid upon us. We start with those areas that God reveals to us and make our stand. As we do, He provides victory and opens our eyes to new areas that need to be fortified and conquered. If we continue the fight, we experience progressive victory over sin, and sanctification becomes a reality in our life and relationship with God! In our humanness, we won't win every skirmish but God promises that *if* we continue to pursue Him and fight the enemy, we *will* win the war and will grow to be more and more like Him!

Defining the battle lines is something the enemy does not want you to do. He will seek to blur the lines and delay you as long as possible because it limits his opportunities to amplify and twist the natural desires of your flesh. He will do his best to continually move the battle lines and reveal holes in the fence in an attempt to maintain access to you. In the book "*The Normal Christian Life*" Watchman Nee relays an interesting story that is applicable here.

"During the first three months of the Japanese war in China we lost a great many tanks and so were unable to deal with the Japanese tanks, until the following scheme was devised. A single shot would be fired at a Japanese tank by one of our snipers in ambush. After a considerable lapse of time the first shot would be followed by a second; then, after a further silence, by another shot; until the tank driver, eager to locate the source of the disturbance, would pop his head out to look around. The next shot, carefully aimed, would put an end to him."

"...Each person is tempted when they are dragged away by their own evil desire and enticed." (James 1:14)

Defining the battle lines is a tangible front line of defense designed to keep us from getting tempted into letting our head go where the enemy has a clear shot! So many times the enemy will introduce a seemingly innocent thought into our mind and we allow it to linger. If we don't take these lesser thoughts captive, they begin to multiply and become the kindling the enemy needs to set us on fire.

"In addition to all this, take up the shield of faith, with which you can extinguish all the flaming arrows of the evil one." (Ephesians 6:13)

Chapter 14 | Enter the Battle (Part 1)

"Get Real" Questions for discussion with other men:

Jesus said anyone who commits sin is a slave to sin (John 8:34) Do you currently "feel" like a slave to sin or a slave of Christ? What is your answer based on?

What first comes to mind when thinking about the area where you may need to draw a battle line to protect you from temptation?

What would be the area that you are most resistant to drawing a battle line? Why are you resistant?

Have you ever taken steps to define the battle lines regarding your temptations? If not, why not?

Authors note: Please consider providing a review of The Purity Driven Life on Amazon.com.

Chapter 15 | Enter the battle – (Part 2)

"The way to love someone is to lightly run your finger over that person's soul until you find a crack, and then gently to pour love into that crack" [1]

"Not neglecting meeting together, as is the habit of some, but encourage each other" (Hebrews 10:25)

Step 3 - Find your band of brothers

Having other Christian men in your life that you can trust is a vital part of the process of defeating sin. Each of these steps is challenging but joining your heart and soul to other Christian men in this fight is crucial for several reasons. Listen to James, the brother of Jesus.

"Confess to one another therefore your faults (your slips, your false steps, your offenses, your sins) and pray [also] for one another, that you may be healed *and* restored [to a spiritual tone of mind and heart]. The earnest (heartfelt, continued) prayer of a righteous man makes tremendous power available [dynamic in its working]." (James 5:16 Amplified version)

Why do we need to do this? I certainly didn't want to confess my weakness and utter depravity to other men and you probably don't either. However, for me personally, it has been one of the greatest experiences of my life. Confession deals with our deep issues of pride and lack of humility. True confession frees us to experience true love. God will use the men he puts in your life to make you a better man if you are willing to submit and embrace this process. Below are four ways that God will use these men to refine you.

> *"...men holding themselves accountable to nobody ought not to be trusted by anybody."*
>
> *~ Thomas Paine ~*

1) We learn to receive love – Those who have hidden sin are not able to receive love because they know that any love offered is *uninformed love*. Most of us aren't consciously aware of this, but on some level we believe "If others only knew about my past...what has been done to me...what I think in my head...the insecurities I hold...how fake I am...the sin I engage in when I am alone... they wouldn't be offering their love to me." As a result, we see the love offered as uninformed, and therefore cannot be trusted or received as dependable, true, or real love.

In the book *"The Cure"* the authors explain why those who hide spiritually are unable to get the love they so desperately crave.

"Because they trust no one, their needs aren't met. Because their needs aren't met, they live out of selfishness. Not only do they not receive love, they don't give it either. In God's eyes, receiving love always comes before giving love…We have heard too many messages on 'learning to love more" or "learning to love better.' In truth, we love only when we first learn how to receive the love of God and others. 'We love because He first loved us.'…Unresolved sin causes us to define our most innate needs as weaknesses. If we see our needs as weaknesses, we'll hide our limitations and call it self-reliance, or we'll pretend we have no needs and call it independence. Or we'll believe that no one should have to meet our needs and call it strength…needs give us the capacity to feel loved. We know or experience love when our needs are met."[2]

For the man with unresolved and unconfessed sin in his life, that sin becomes a blockage preventing him from receiving real love from God or man. His heart has become hardened by his sin and he turns inward, becoming increasingly prideful and selfish. This is why God hates pride. It is through the process of surrender to God in humility, confession, *and* accountability that God is able to remove the blockage and we are able to receive his love directly and through his people.

God loves us so much, and as we humble ourselves and confess our sin to others, we are able to receive his love and healing. Then, and only then, can his love begin to flow through us to others in community. We are then able to love and pray for others to receive the healing that has come upon us. Our prayers truly become powerful because they are motivated by the love of God flowing through us!

2) ***Humility is developed*** - By being part of a true accountability group our pride is subjected to humility. Getting the upper hand on pride requires exposing sin through confession, not just to God but also to other men. Hiding our sin makes us weak. Being real, open, and honest makes us vulnerable and humble, but *ultimately* it makes us stronger and *spiritually effective and powerful* in God's Kingdom! This is a very powerful truth, for God promises that healing from our sin comes through this path of humility and confession. Pride is the dominate power behind our flesh and our temptation to sin. The only way to crush it is to expose our sin and weakness through humility and confession. Again, as our sin is confessed and exposed, God promises that our prayers become powerful and effective as his love can begin to flow through us. This is how God, our amazingly wise Father designed it.

The principle of exposure

Luke 6 tells of an occasion where Jesus went into the synagogue to teach. As He taught, he saw in the crowd a man with a withered hand. During this time, many believed that sickness and deformities were a curse from God for personal sinfulness. I imagine this man tried to keep his useless, withered hand hidden from sight and under his robes as much as possible. Maybe, in listening to Jesus teach he forgot himself and let his guard down, exposing his hand. All we know is that the text says Jesus saw his withered hand. Jesus said to the man,

"...Get up and stand in front of everyone." So he got up and stood there. Then Jesus ... said to the man,

"Stretch out your hand." He did so, and his hand was completely restored." (Luke 6:6-10)

Jesus called the man to come forward and expose his hand, and as the man obeyed, his hand was healed. I am sure this was not a comfortable act of obedience for this man. But through confession, this principle of exposure is how God has chosen to heal our sin. As we commit to an accountability group and begin to open our lives to other men, we are able to confess and expose our sin, and healing begins to take place. Our ability to sense God's love and care in our lives is renewed as our hearts are softened and compassion for others blossoms.

We cannot continue to hide our sin and weaknesses and expect to receive the healing that God has for us. Like so many biblical truths this may not seem to be logical, but there is strength in humbling ourselves and doing this God's way.

3) We begin to hear God - Sin blocks our ability to hear God's voice and sense his presence. When we humble ourselves and set our pride aside, we begin to be able to hear God speaking to us through whatever mouth He chooses to speak. Being in an accountability group gives God the opportunity to speak to us on a regular basis as we get real about our struggles and weaknesses with other Christian men.

All of us are tempted and have weak points in our character. We all are in need of others to help us see clearly. Those in a true accountability group who have dealt, and are dealing with sexual sin, will not allow us to continue deceiving ourselves.

Proverbs 15:22 tells us "there is wisdom in the counsel of many."

It is humbling yet wise to surround ourselves with other men who are looking out for our spiritual well-being, our marriages and our integrity.

Humility brings healing

In 2 Kings, Naaman, a very powerful man and the commander of the armies of the King of Aram has leprosy. It turns out that there was a young Israelite slave girl working in his home who told Naaman's wife about a prophet of God named Elisha. This Israelite girl claimed that Elisha could cure Naaman of his disease if he will go see him.

Naaman makes the journey and shows up at Elisha's house in fanfare with his entourage, but Elisha doesn't bother to come out to greet him or even invite him into his home to discuss why he has come. Instead, Elisha, already knowing why Naaman has come, sends his servant to the door with a message, telling Naaman that if he will go dip himself in the Jordan River seven times then his health will be restored.

This is an amazing test of Naaman's ability to humble himself and set his pride aside. First, Elisha didn't give him the respect he believed a man of his stature deserved. Elisha didn't even acknowledge Naaman's arrival with a personal greeting. Second, Elisha sends a lowly servant out to relay the instructions for his healing, further demeaning him in front of his staff and troops. Third, Naaman is told to go take a bath in the muddy local tributary. This might have involved him getting undressed in front of all of his subordinates. Needless to say, Naaman is offended. However, on the advice and urging of his men, Naaman follows Elisha's instructions and is healed.

The beauty of regularly attending an accountability group is that you will receive healing suggestions and wisdom from men you never would have met or trusted outside of this type of relationship. Sometimes you will not like the wisdom shared, but it is an excellent opportunity to humble yourself and recognize that God is working through these men to help you. The other incredible thing that happens is that as you heal and experience God's grace and victory, you get to be used by God. He will use you to speak his healing and encouragement into the lives of other men who come into your group, broken and desperate for someone to help them walk where you have already been. It is the love of Christ in action, and you get to participate!

John Piper in talking about why the Church needs small groups in addition to Church attendance is equally applicable to our need for a band of brothers and is summarized below. [3]

- Hiding in a congregation, we can more easily evade moments of apparent conviction.

- Wise men around us can gently provoke discussion in a safe environment, but in a large worship setting you can just walk away without it taking root. An accountability group provides opportunity for questions leading to growth.

- There is a powerful impulse to avoid painful growth by hiding in the congregation. The tendency toward passivity is part of our human weakness, and other men can prod us to avoid becoming passive and urge us to continue to act in integrity, even under difficult circumstances.

- Congregational settings tend to be poor settings for accountability in personal application. The sermon may touch a nerve of conviction, but without someone to press in, it can easily be avoided.

- Accountability for follow-through on good resolve happens in an accountability group. If your band of brothers knows what you intend to do, the resolve is stronger.

- Prayer support for a specific need or conviction or resolve is available. O how many blessings we do not have because we are not surrounded by a band of brothers who pray for us.

4) We develop trust - When I first started this journey, I never anticipated the level of love and loyalty I would feel for the men in my groups. We developed relationships not around bravado, sports, or politics but around our desire to please God by conquering sin and our willingness to be honest and vulnerable. These types of relationships are rare among men and not without reason.

So many men have deep father wounds that contribute to a propensity toward sexual sin. No matter what our age, down deep we long for our fathers to love us regardless of what we have done. We crave to know that we made him proud, that he thought we were competent and grew up to be a real man in his eyes. Unfortunately, many of us feel like we could never live up to our father's expectations. Our worth was only acknolwledged as we excelled at work, sports, grades or maybe just by staying out of dad's way. Because of this, the relationship never became an authentic relationship where our fathers really shared themselves with us. Consequently, we never truly knew our fathers and they never truly knew who we were either.

In an accountability group, you will share your deepest sins and weaknesses in a place where you are accepted and loved as a fellow warrior pursuing God. In accountability, we are able to experience relationships with other men that most of us never experienced with our fathers or in the world where competitive conquest is the norm. Most men have lived on their own emotionally and spiritually for so long they don't even recognize the need or see the potential benefit of this type of relationship. I know I didn't.

> *"God is ready to assume full responsibility for the life wholly yielded to Him"*
>
> *~ Andrew Murray ~*

A moment of epiphany

After I had been in a group for about a year, I was having great success in walking well and my relationship with God had come alive like never before. We were in group one night when one of the guys shared something. I don't even remember what it was, but I had an epiphany! It was so clear that it shocked me that I had never seen it before! I realized that one of the main drivers causing me to pursue women (and sex) in an unhealthy way was an effort to make up for the lack of authentic male relationships in my life, starting with my father. Now that I had established trusting and honest relationships with other men, for the first time in my life, much of my desire for inappropriate sex had simply disappeared.

I was truly amazed and I now understand why the enemy works so hard to destroy men. If he can cause men to distrust each other and avoid the vulnerability of real male relationships, he keeps us isolated and snared in bondage, unable to hear God's voice. Through this strategy, he gains access to our wives and children, and has entry to destroy our families and future generations!

Step 4 - Recruit a Sniper if needed

Sometimes, depending on the level of our woundedness it becomes apparent that there is need for a skilled professional to help us target and take out deep enemy strongholds that continue to evade our efforts. In addition, there may be medical and mental factors that contribute to our unhealthy behaviors that may require the education and wisdom of a professional counselor.

This is another area where many men just don't want to lay aside their pride and seek help. One of the best pieces of advice I got from my first mentor is that a good counselor, no matter how expensive, is cheaper than the financial and emotional destruction caused to your life and family by continued bondage to sin and/or divorce.

A good Christian counselor who understands sexual issues is worth their weight in gold and is a godly ministry unto itself. I cannot stress enough how helpful they can be in this process. In an accountability group, you can find referrals to a good counselor from those in your group who have experienced success. If you need a counselor, I urge you to seek a referral from a person who has worked with a counselor to *successfully* overcome addiction issues in their life. There are many ineffective counselors out there and you want to be wise with your time and money. Recall my example of trying to buy the cheap flea killer for my cat. All I did was prolong the battle until I was willing to pay for the good stuff.

A good counselor will help you expose wounds you are likely not aware of, connect the dots, and then help you experience forgiveness and take responsibility as you move forward. They can provide you specific tasks and exercises to help strengthen areas of weakness and recognize patterns of behavior that cause you to unknowingly engage in self-destructive behavior. They can recommend books, education, and additional tools for success tailored to your situation. I personally found the counselor I used to be a crucial weapon in this fight, and just one more area of accountability as I learned to walk without depending on sexual sin for comfort.

Step 5 - Active Defense and Advance Forces

1 Corinthians 10:4-6 says "The weapons we fight with are not the weapons of the world. On the contrary, they have *divine power* to demolish strongholds. We demolish arguments and every pretension that sets itself up against the knowledge of God, and we take captive every thought to make it obedient to Christ."

To fight effectively we need to know about the weapons at our disposal. This fight is a spiritual one and the Bible says we have spiritual weapons that have divine power capable of demolishing thoughts and arguments that come against our knowledge of God. Beyond the armor listed in Ephesians 6, what are some of these weapons?

The Holy Spirit – Our most powerful weapon is the appropriation of the power of the Holy Spirit. The blood of Jesus pays the penalty for our sin. The resurrection makes the Holy Spirit available for us to have power to walk the new life. A man who has invited the Holy Spirit to fill him and lead in his life is a powerful weapon in the hand of God. This is a daily invitation and yielding. All the other Spiritual weapons are only partially effective in the hand of a man not willing to submit to the Spirit of Christ (Acts 1:8). This is a study unto itself and there are a great number of books written on the subject from various angles and theologies, but one I found particularly instrumental in my own life was *"Surprised by the power of the Spirit"* By Jack Deere. It came in answer to prayer as I was pursuing this topic in my own growth.

"Every man is as full of the Holy Spirit as he wants to be. He may not be as full as he wishes he were, but he is most certainly as full as he wants to be."

~ A.W. Tozer ~

Knowledge of the God's word – How can we take captive thoughts and arguments that come against our knowledge of God if we have none? This is the very foundation of our faith, and without diligently seeking to know God's word we will limp along at best (John 8:32). However, understanding the word of God is predicated on our dependence of the Holy Spirit to discern and understand it (1 Corinthians 2:14).

The choice to believe – Jesus, by his death, has purchased your freedom to align your will with his and the power of the Holy Spirit as a witness to his grace; however, you also have the freedom to hand your will over to the enemy of your soul. Every day God will allow you the opportunity to choose to believe his word, and act in faith, or to pursue an alternative. In this sense, you control your daily destiny through your free will, and your acceptance of the consequences (Galatians 6:7, 8).

Prayer – There is tremendous power in the prayer of the saints. Even though God knows what we need before we ask, it is through discerning his will and the asking that we become partakers of his nature and are formed to his likeness. (1 John 5:14) This is another great topic for ongoing study. I have been greatly helped by the book *"Andrew Murray on Prayer."* It is a compilation of several works by Andrew Murray that I have used as a devotional for many years.

Gratitude – Thanksgiving and praise are the natural outcome of believing that God loves us, and if we are surrendered to him he works all things together for our good, no matter what we are facing, no matter how big the giant appears (1 Thessalonians 5:18). Thanksgiving and gratitude should be practiced daily to counter our enemy's attacks. Covetousness or lust is a desire for what we do not have. Gratitude is thankfulness for what God has provided and entrusted to us. If we trust Him as a loving Father then we will be grateful for what He has provided, believing that He knows what is best for us. If that is true, then we are right where God wants us (for the moment), and He will supply our needs in his perfect timing.

Vigilant awareness - When things are going good our natural tendency is to let down the defenses just a little bit, but one of the great things about being in an accountability group is that when things are going good you will be encouraged to use this time to prepare for the next attack of the enemy.

1 Peter 5:8 says, "Be alert and of sober mind. Your enemy the devil prowls around like a roaring lion looking for someone to devour."

In times of ease or victory, we need to be vigilant and watchful for the next attack, and use this time to encourage others who are under attack. When it comes to fighting, some battles are small skirmishes that are down and dirty but end quickly as the enemy flees. Others are prolonged campaigns as the enemy is entrenched and proves difficult to dislodge. I want to encourage you to vow to never, never give up the fight.

Galatians 6:9 promises us this. "Let us not become weary in doing good, for at the proper time we will reap a harvest if we do not give up."

Step 6 – Help other POW's escape

I know that as you read this you may be at a very difficult time in your life. You may even be at a point of despair, just as I was when I started this beautiful, painful, and blissful journey. It may seem impossible to you that God could ever take the shattered pieces of your life and bring you to a place of happiness and peace again, much less use you to help others escape what you are now caught in, but I promise you, it can happen if you just trust Jesus to lead you.

God will take what is left of the wreckage of your life and multiply his healing touch through you to become his hands in touching the lives of others. It is the most unexpected benefit of this beautiful process. Not only do we get a real and tangible relationship with Jesus, and all the benefits that come with it; we get to take the hand of others and lead them to our precious savior who takes them in his arms and begins to lead them on their own personal journey of intimacy and healing.

"As I have loved you, love one another" (John 15:12)

Chapter 15 | Enter the Battle (Part 2)

"Get Real" Questions for discussion with other men:

Would you be willing to join a band of brothers to whom you can be vulnerable and honestly confess your sins and faults? Are you *eager* or simply *willing* to join one? Why did you answer this way?

In assessing yourself, would you say you are able to receive love from other men and from God?

If you said "yes," does it flow through you or are you deceiving yourself? How do you know?

John Piper talks about hiding in the congregation, being moved by a sermon but never taking action. Have you done this? How will this change in your life?

If you are not proactively engaged in preparing your "active defense and advance forces," why not? What needs to change?

Chapter 16 | Abiding

"Our rest lies in looking to the Lord, not to ourselves."[1]

God, you have made us for yourself, and our hearts are restless till they find their rest in you."[2]

"Come to me, all you who are weary and burdened, and I will give you rest." (Matthew 11:28)

As I close this book, I want to share a personal story. Just an analogy to reinforce a point I made earlier.

Recently, I was placed in charge of an initiative to begin figuring out how to utilize video for marketing, education, and information within our company. This isn't an area that falls within my skillset or experience, but since there was no one else more qualified, the assignment fell to me. I began the research process and within a month, I selected the equipment that fit our facility and the type of projects we would be doing. I put together the proposal, presented it, and received the approval to move forward.

I ordered the equipment and started working with the building manager to make the necessary upgrades to the audiovisual systems in our conference center to ensure they would work properly with the new equipment. While this was going on, the equipment began arriving and it was all very exciting. We had scheduled a guest speaker who would be flying in from out of town for a big presentation in a few weeks and it looked like we would be ready just in time to record the event.

The weekend before the event, I was in the office testing the equipment. I read the manual to make sure I would have enough memory for recording the three hour event. I researched the lighting. I practiced the shot for the right framing. I tried out the various camera filters. I made sure the camera was set to capture the recording in the right format and compression. There was a lot to know and I wanted to make sure this went off without a hiccup.

The day of the event, I couldn't sleep and was up at 3 am. I did my devotions and arrived at the office early to set everything up and go over all the parameters one more time. I wanted to make sure I hadn't forgotten anything. By the time the event started, I was ready. Sound? Check! Filters? Check! Power? Check! Frame? Check! Lighting? Check! It wasn't until I went to upload the film later that day that I realized I never pushed the "record" button!

I had meticulously gone over all the secondary items but neglected the one crucial thing, pushing the "record" button. I could have made mistakes on the secondary's and still captured the event, possibly being able to fix them in editing. But when you don't push the "record" button all you get is a big load of nothing! There was no fix and no second chance. All the invested time and activity was for nothing because the most crucial thing was overlooked.

When it comes to your battle with sin, you can exercise all diligence in the secondary's, but if you neglect the foundation of pursuing a living relationship with Jesus Christ you will have no rest in this world, and you will have nothing in the end. There is no second chance. Nothing else matters unless it is built on the foundation of a relationship with Jesus Christ.

Staying connected

Jesus uses an analogy from the vineyard, saying we are the branches and He is the vine. For a branch to produce fruit, it has to be connected to receive the life that flows from and through the vine. For a branch to stay alive, it must stay connected. There is no such thing as a part-time branch. If it becomes disconnected, it dies.

What isn't immediately clear but is also true, is that the vine cannot bear the fruit without the branch. They must be in unison. I said this before but it is worth remembering. We cannot produce fruit, overcome sin, change our desires, etc. without God, but He will not do it apart from our participation. This is the position in which God has placed Himself in relation to us.

2 Corinthians 4:6 says, "For God, who said, 'Let light shine out of darkness,' made his light shine in our hearts to give us the light of the knowledge of God's glory displayed in the face of Christ."

We are to reflect God, and we can only do that when our hearts are fully connected in relationship with Jesus.

In the book *"Waiting on Christ"* Andrew Murray uses a beautiful analogy in relation to this verse that I just love.

"Just as the sun shines its beautiful, life-giving light on and into our earth, so God shines into our hearts the light of His glory, of His love, in Christ His Son. Our heart is meant to have that light filling and gladdening it all the day… Those beautiful trees and flowers, with all this green grass, what do they do to keep the sun shining on them? They do nothing; they simply bask in the sunshine, when it comes. The sun is millions of miles away, but over all that distance it comes, its own light and joy; and the tiniest flower that lifts its little head upwards is met by the same exuberance of light and blessing as flood the widest landscape. We have not to care for the light we need for our day's work; the sun cares, and provides and shines the light around us all the day. We simply count upon it, and receive it, and enjoy it."

"The only difference between nature and grace is this, that what the trees and the flowers do unconsciously, as they drink in the blessing of the light, is to be with us a voluntary and a loving acceptance. Faith, simple faith in God's word and love, is to be the opening of the eyes, the opening of the heart, to receive and enjoy the unspeakable glory of His grace. And just as the trees, day by day, and month by month, stand and grow into beauty and fruitfulness, just welcoming whatever sunshine the sun may give, so it is the very highest exercise of our Christian life just to abide in the light of

God, and let it, and let Him, fill us with the life and the brightness it brings."[3]

I can just see in my mind's eye the little leafy plant opening its leaves to the sun as it rises; stretching upward, facing its tender leaves to soak up the golden rays. As the sun travels through the sky, the hungry little plant bends its body to follow the path of the sun until at last, the day closes and he folds up his fragile leaves in thankful gratitude, to sleep until tomorrow. What a beautiful picture of the life of the victorious Christian, eyes ever on Jesus, straining to hear his gentle whisper, sensitive to his presence and sweet call to be mindful of his constant care and love shining upon us throughout the day.

This is a place of *daily* repentance and submission to God, our eyes ever upon his beauty and love for us. This is a place where we embrace in daily confession that we are broken and prideful. Then, willingly choose to face the day God's way, whatever the cost. This is a place of victory over sin, this is abiding in Christ. There is no "formula" for this place of relationship; it really is a "heart thing" that must start with a genuine, sincere "come to Jesus" meeting which includes an honest confession of sin.

For me, it started with a very honest conversation with God. I found myself saying and praying something much like this every day.

"God, I know something is broken in me. My sin doesn't even make me feel guilty anymore. I can barely hear the conviction of the Holy Spirit. I know that my sin must break your heart, but I can't stop. I do love you but I am powerless to live the life you called me to. I ask that you begin to do a work in my heart and allow me to *feel* in my heart and spirit what you feel when I sin against you. Allow me to feel the pain I cause you."

As I write this, tears are streaming down my face because it was only a few months until God answered this prayer. As I began to pray this every day, I started to get really serious about addressing the sexual sin in my life. It wasn't long before I had two to three months of abstinence from pornography and I was feeling proud of myself for my exercise of "willpower." I literally remember thinking *"I think I have this thing licked!"* Looking back, it was a pride-filled statement. Rather than giving credit to God, I was congratulating myself on the success of *my* efforts. A few days later that I stumbled back into sin, and my heart was broken with the pain of what I had done. I broke down in full body sobs, feeling the pain of recognizing my pride and the betrayal of my Savior. I will never forget that day. It was a turning point in the battle because I realized the absolute depth of my dependence and need for daily reliance on my Savior if I was ever to walk this Christian life.

> *"It is not that we need more power, but that we need more brokenness. When we are properly broken we will find the indwelling Christ is more than sufficient."*
>
> *~ Chip Brogden ~*

It was a very humbling moment. I imagine my sudden awareness and pain to be, in some small way, like the Apostle Peter's when the rooster crowed and he realized the extent of his weakness and utter sinfulness. In retrospect, I am so very grateful for that moment because I never want to experience hurting my Jesus like that again. He showed me that I cannot have victory over sin without humility and continual dependence on Him.

One last reminder as I close. I have said it before but I want to make sure no one misunderstands. This battle with sin and our relationship with God is not about perfection, but pursuit. We were made to pursue God and love Him with all of our heart. My desire is that this book does not bring condemnation, but instead produces a conviction and encouragement that leads to biblical repentance. Without repentance we are not given access to the grace of Jesus. Repentance is evidenced by embracing humility, confessing our sin, and acknowledging our need for the crucifixion of Christ. When we do this daily, we choose to become a weapon in the hand of our Savior in the victory over our sin. Read the following verses slowly.

"If we deliberately keep on sinning after we have received the knowledge of the truth, no sacrifice for sins is left, but only the fearful expectation of judgment and the raging fire that will consume the enemies of God." (Hebrews 10:26)

"Put to death, therefore, whatever belongs to your earthly nature: sexual immorality, impurity, lust, evil desires and greed, which is idolatry." (Colossians 3:5)

"One final word, my friends. We ask you—*urge* is more like it—that you keep doing what we told you to do in order to please God, not in a dogged religious plod, but in a living, spirited dance. You know the guidelines we laid out for you from the Master Jesus. God wants you to live a pure life. **Keep yourselves from sexual promiscuity.** Learn to appreciate and give dignity to your body, not abusing it, as is so common among those who know nothing of God. We've warned you about this before. God hasn't invited us into a disorderly, unkempt life, but into something holy and beautiful—as beautiful on the inside as the outside. *If you disregard this advice, you're not offending your neighbors; you're rejecting God,* who is making you a gift of his Holy Spirit." (1 Thessalonians 4:1-8 The Message)

Won't you join with me and other men in this battle to pursue God and become the mighty men of God we are called to be? Are you ready to get radical in dealing with your sin? Are you ready to fight for your family, your wife and children? Are you willing to become the spotless bride of Christ? If so, this means absolute surrender to Christ and engaging in an all-out war on the giants in the land.

Fight! Every. Day.

Chapter 16 | Abiding

"Get Real" Questions for discussion with other men:

Have you joined a men's accountability group yet?

Does your Church have a venue for getting into an accountability group?

Will you take the steps to start an accountability group at your Church if there isn't one?

How can you facilitate a conversation about the struggles Christian men in your Church face?

What is the next step the Holy Spirit is directing you to take?

A note to shepherds of God's flock

"Not many of you should become teachers, my brothers; for you know that we who teach will be judged with a greater strictness." (James 3:1)

As I was praying about how to address the pastors who will read this book, the Holy Spirit reminded me of an episode from my past. I think it carries a powerful object lesson applicable to God's call on pastors to preach the entire word of God to his people.

When I was young and unsaved, I found myself dating several women at the same time. I had become sexually involved with one of the women. I will call her Darla. In an effort to "display" some honesty, I assured her that now that we were sleeping together our relationship would be "monogamous."

I chose to define monogamous as "not sleeping with anyone else," but I still planned to continue seeing other women. I wanted to keep my options open, but didn't want Darla to *think* I was anything less than completely honest. I felt fortunate that Darla never asked for clarification of my definition but, as I hoped, she assumed that my definition was the same as hers. She was under the impression that we had defined the relationship as completely exclusive; even though I knew that was not the case.

About a month later, I went out with a young lady named Sarah, one of the other girls I had continued to see. The next day when I was talking on the phone with Darla, she asked, "What did you do last night?" I said, "Oh, nothing much. I just hung out with Sarah."

At the time, I was living with a platonic female roommate who also happened to have the name of Sarah. Darla assumed wrongly that I spent the previous evening with my roommate Sarah and didn't question me any further.

I could have answered Darla's question by saying, "Oh, I went on a date last night." Both statements are true. I had spent the evening with Sarah and I had gone on a date. However, these two small statements would have radically different meaning to Darla. The second would have generated a vastly different response, but because Darla had *incomplete* information, filtered through her personal frame of reference, the implications of my words were missed.

To Darla, the first sentence caused no sense of concern. She did not feel rejection or jealousy. Based on her interpretation of my words, there was no information requiring her to make a change in our relationship or have any doubts about us. The second sentence would have provoked an immediate, emotional response. She would have felt a sense of rejection and betrayal. Knowing that I had spent the evening with another woman would most certainly have changed our relationship!

I justified my answer to Darla's question as "technically" truthful. I had said the "words" that truthfully told her who I had spent the previous evening with BUT, I had purposely chosen to "package" my answer in a way that would minimize her negative reaction. *I hoped to minimize the possibility of her rejecting me.* If she misunderstood, was that my fault?

What I realize now is that I was completely responsible for Darla's misunderstanding and misinterpreting the reality of the situation. Any normal person would have assumed I was talking about my roommate. By packaging the message the way I did, I withheld information that I *knew, if spelled out clearly, would have altered her choices.* Those choices would have resulted in the end of our relationship.

Out of pride and selfishness, I chose to communicate in such a way as to allow Darla to come to her own conclusions. At that point, I chose to believe the ball of responsibility was now in her court. In reality, I had deceived her for fear of losing her affirmation and sexual attention. The result was good for me (from a sinful standpoint) and bad for her. My actions were motivated by fear and love of self.

God gave me this example to share because my actions toward Darla are mirrored by many pastors in how they communicate with the congregations God has entrusted them with. These pastors have allowed the congregation to reach conclusions about sin that are not biblical. Look at the evidence. Polls show that

approximately 75% of Americans claim to be Christian,[1] yet:
- 56% of Americans support gay marriage[2]
- 65% of Americans are pro-choice.[3]
- 60% of men, (50% of pastors) and 30% of women sitting in the Church are addicted to or struggling with pornography, erotica and sexual sin.[4]
- The Church has nearly the same divorce rate as our culture.[5]

Is this the bride of Christ, who will be presented before Him in splendor without spot or wrinkle, holy without blemish? (Ephesians 5:27)

No, it is not.

What has happened in the Church is largely the result of watering down the Gospel in an effort to be seeker friendly. What started as trying to be less "hellfire and brimstone" and more culturally attractive has turned into a "gospel" of easy grace. Congregations are attracted to a feel good message that rarely leads to true repentance or deliverance from sin.

Many pastors have been serving up a message of grace and prosperity, while avoiding talk of blood, sanctification, and the need for deliverance from sin for fear of offending and losing attendees. The measure of a "healthy" Church has become the size of the congregation rather than the spiritual condition of the flock.

If 50% of pastors are addicted to pornography and see no need to fight personal sin, how can they lead the sheep or expect his people to live holy lives? As one pastor put it, "I was in a six month affair, at the same time preaching and counseling against adultery, and telling myself that God didn't care because the Church was growing."[6]

A.W. Tozer writes in *"The Crucified Life,"*

"We have come to our present low state as a result of an almost fanatical emphasis on grace to the total exclusion of obedience, self-discipline, patience, personal holiness, cross carrying discipleship and other such precious doctrines in the Church."

We have lost faith in the convicting Spirit of God as the compelling factor in bringing someone to repentance and a true relationship with God. We have substituted winsomeness, wit, and a warm atmosphere, fueled by our desire for success as the modern Church world defines it. God defines success as a flock that is healthy and disease free; as a group of individuals who deny the flesh out of love for Him. The Church of Jesus is meant to be a bride longing for the groom's presence, preparing herself with great detail for her expectant wedding day.

The only way the Church could arrive at the state we are in today is if the majority of the shepherds are fulfilling 1 Timothy 4:3 and teaching what the people want to hear rather than the entire range of the word. A dear pastor friend used to say,

"We all love dessert but you have to serve the full meal first, and that includes the vegetables or we all get sick."[7]

The job of the shepherd is to care for the sheep, to ensure their health and rescue them from danger. Pastors are called to teach the whole word of God clearly, so that the sheep cannot walk away uninformed or misunderstanding the consequence of sin. If the message isn't clearly preached, and the sheep don't understand grace AND the requirement for heart repentance, the sheep are not at fault, the pastor is! The word says faith comes by hearing. They cannot hear it if you do not preach it.

The call to pastor is a holy calling. You are a man entrusted to participate with the Spirit of God in preparing the bride of Christ for her wedding day. You are responsible for the teaching and care of his flock. If the flock has ticks, burrs and matted fur, and is sickly from drinking bad water, it is your job when they are entrusted to your care, to lovingly clean them up and heal them so they don't contaminate the rest of the sheep. Quoting from Chris Braun's' book, *"Unpacking Forgiveness"*:

"Tragedies of 'cheap grace' are multiple. First, there is a large group of people who think they are Christians when they are not. A second negative consequence of 'cheap grace' is that the believers fail to think discerningly about what is right and wrong. When evil is not identified and named it soon flourishes."

- Are your sheep diseased with sexual sin and divorce?
- Do they have lenient attitudes that *excuse* continued sin under the guise of grace?
- What have you done to warn your sheep about the consequences of continuing to walk in sin?
- Have you sought to provide avenues of help and support for them to overcome and deal with these sins?
- Or have you chosen to avoid calling sin, sin and wash your hands of the responsibility?
- Is your leadership sending the message that you believe sin doesn't matter because we are under grace?
- Does preaching boldly against the sins of this age cause a pang of fear in you?
- What would God have you to do?

Pastor, if you are called of God to preach, you were born for this time and place in history. If you love Him, FEED HIS SHEEP... the whole word of God.

And the Lord replied, "A faithful, sensible servant is one to whom the master can give the responsibility of managing his other household servants and feeding them." Luke 12:42

Resources

Visit www.thepuritydrivenlife.org for more resources

https://www.facebook.com/thepuritydrivenlife

If this book has impacted you, please write by visiting the website and let me know what God is doing in your life, your marriage and your Church. Your testimony can be a great source of encouragement to other men who are deep in the battle. Also, if you haven't already, would you consider reviewing this book on Amazon.com?

FOOTNOTES

Chapter 1
1. Brennan Manning, The Ragamuffin Gospel; Good news for the Bedraggled, Beat-up, and Burnt out
2. washingtonian.com/blogs/wellbeing/health/the-most-popular-cosmetic-surgery-in-2011-was.php
3. www.surgery.org/consumers/plastic-surgery-news-briefs/cosmetic-surgery--15-years-facts-figures
4. www.yahoo.com/knock-off-knock-20m-fake-designer-goods-seized-181950657--abc-news-topstories.html
5. I highly recommend this series. More information can be found at http://kingdommanbook.com/

Chapter 2
1. Jim Elliott, Quotes

Chapter 3
1. Oswald Chambers, Quotes
2. George McDonald, Quotes
3. transparentministries.org/porn-stats/
4. http://www.hrsa.gov/hansensdisease/dataandstatistics.html

Chapter 4
1. I could find no original author. If none arise, credit goes to the Holy Spirit.

Chapter 5
1. Fred Allen, Quotes
2. dailymail.co.uk/tvshowbiz/article-176598/Do-worship-celebs.html
3. I read this somewhere and wrote it down because I was so shocked but I couldn't relocate the reference. If anyone is aware please send me the reference so can give credit.
4. I heard this in a sermon by Tony Evans but could remember the exact message.

Chapter 6

1. Garbage in, garbage out - The first use of the term has been dated to a 1 April 1963 in a syndicated newspaper article about the first stages of computerization of the US Internal Revenue Service. The term was brought to prominence as a teaching mantra by George Fuechsel, an IBM 305 RAMAC technician/instructor in New York. - Source Wikipedia
2. A common paraphrase of "Tell me what you eat and I will tell you what you are." attributed to French lawyer and politician Jean Anthelme Brillat-Savarin (died 1826) – Source Wikipedia
3. Sexpresso? Seattle-Area Coffee 'Cowgirls' Show Skin to Get Business, Jan 29, 2007 Associated Press
4. So many great resources on the web for information on Pavlov and classical conditioning.
5. From my memory related to a sermon I once heard. I searched the web but couldn't find a reference.

Chapter 7
1. Bonnell Thornton, Quotes

Chapter 8
1. Randy Alcorn, Quotes

Chapter 9
1. Watchman Nee, God's Keeping Powerfully, Quotes

Chapter 10
1. Dietrich Bonheoffer, The Cost of Discipleship

Chapter 11
1. William Faulkner, As I lay dying, Quotes

Chapter 12
1. Watchman Nee, The Normal Christian Life, Deliverance from Sin and the Soul Life

Chapter 13
1. Neil T. Anderson, Quotes
2. These questions come from my listening to the many sermons and teachings of Pastor John Piper and I attribute

them to him. I don't believe these questions are a direct quote but possibly a summation of some type.

Chapter 14
1. Dietrich Bonheoffer, Quotes
2. http://www.youtube.com/watch?v=IHdJVzYBBOU

Chapter 15
1. Keith Miller, Quotes
2. John Lynch, Bruce McNicol, Bill Thrall, The Cure
3. John Piper, "The love of human praise as the root of unbelief" Sept. 20, 2009 (Sermon)

Chapter 16
1. Watchman Nee, The Spiritual Man
2. St. Augustine, Quotes
3. Andrew Murray "Waiting on God" Chapter 16

A note to shepherds of God's flock
1. http://en.wikipedia.org/wiki/Religion_in_the_United_States
2. http://en.wikipedia.org/wiki/Public_opinion_of_same-sex_marriage_in_the_United_States#By_religion
3. http://www.gallup.com/poll/162548/americans-misjudge-abortion-views.aspx
4. www.transparentministries.org/porn-stats/
5. http://www.barna.org/family-kids-articles/42-new-marriage-and-divorce-statistics-released?q=divorce
6. www.desiringgod.org/blog/posts/sexual-sin-in-the-ministry
7. Pastor Robert Wood

Made in the USA
Charleston, SC
09 November 2016